COLLEGE SURVIVAL
FOR STUDENT-ATHLETES

COLLEGE SURVIVAL
FOR STUDENT-ATHLETES

By

GEORGE HENDERSON, Ph.D.

S.N. Goldman Professor of Human Relations
and
Professor of Education
University of Oklahoma
Norman, Oklahoma

and

JEROME C. WEBER, Ph.D.

Vice Provost for Instructional Services
and
Dean of the University College
University of Oklahoma
Norman, Oklahoma

CHARLES C THOMAS • PUBLISHER
Springfield • Illinois • U.S.A.

Published and Distributed Throughout the World by

CHARLES C THOMAS • PUBLISHER

2600 South First Street

Springfield, Illinois 62717

© *1985 by* CHARLES C THOMAS • PUBLISHER

ISBN 0-398-05097-X

Library of Congress Catalog Card Number: 84-24044

With THOMAS BOOKS *careful attention is given to all details of manufacturing and
design. It is the Publisher's desire to present books that are satisfactory as to their physical
qualities and artistic possibilities and appropriate for their particular use.* THOMAS
BOOKS *will be true to those laws of quality that assure a good name and good will.*

Printed in the United States of America
PS-R-3

Library of Congress Cataloging in Publication Data

Henderson, George, 1932-
    College survival for student-athletes.

    Bibliography: p.
    Includes index.
    1. College student orientation. 2. Athletes —
Education (Higher). I. Weber, Jerome C. II. Title.
LB2343.3H46 1985   378'.198   84-24044
ISBN 0-398-05097-X

FOREWORD

Athletics as education can be understood as a set of key contributions to the individual, to the institution, and to society at large. Among these contributions are the development of discipline, teamwork, and the self-confidence of individuals who participate in athletics: the improvement and sustenance of institutional reputations and morale, and the heightening of visibility that demonstrably aids in recruitment of students and financial contributions. Varsity athletics provide a stimulus to the development of broad based physical education and intramural athletic programs that contribute to the physical well-being of students. College athletics also have a public service role in satisfying the need or desire for spectator sports expressed by the general public in the stadiums and gymnasiums of colleges and universities across the nation. Recent studies of the sociological, psychological and cultural role of sports make clear its importance to our society.

This quotation is part of a statement on "Athletics as Education" which was approved by the Interassociational Presidents' Committee on Collegiate Athletics in the spring of 1984 and represents the feeling of all major higher education and athletic associations. It is precisely because the authors also believe so strongly in the value of both athletics and education, as well as the fragile relationship which exists between them, that we have undertaken the task of attempting to provide useful information for prospective college level student-athletes. We hope that our advice and perspectives will prove useful to the young men and women now playing high school athletics who are the current and future recruits for college-level participation. It is our intention that this information will allow you to make the best decision in each individual case, meaning that decision which allows you to combine joyful and satisfying athletic participation with productive and meaningful academic activity. While the glory of athletics may be of primary consideration to you today, it is the academic productivity and preparation which will form the basis for your future professional lives. Athletics and academics do not have to exist in ways that are mutually exclusive, and your goal should be to combine these two important activities in ways that allow you the fullest development of your talents and desires.

G. H.
J.C.W.

v

PREFACE

This is a book for student-athletes to read in high school and to take with them to college. It is a **survival manual.** College can be one of the most enjoyable experiences, or it can be one of the most unpleasant. The major reasons for attending college should be to learn academic subjects and to earn a degree. No student should go to college in order to "major" in playing a sport, but many do. Nor should a student attend college in order to major in partying, but many do. The college experience is best when students engage in balanced academic-sports-recreational activities, and the opportunity to achieve this balance should be the foremost factor in selecting a specific school.

We have tried to be objective about college life and thereby help student-athletes to evaluate institutions on the basis of their curriculum, library, housing, and several other things that comprise higher education. In the end, it is neither the athletic facilities nor the academic buildings that make a college an enjoyable and meaningful place. Instead, it is the interactions with people—in and out of sports—that are most important. Throughout this book, we emphasize the *student* part of "student-athlete."

Getting into a college is only the beginning of the higher education process. Staying in and graduating comprise the other aspects. Too many student-athletes attend college as if they were going through a revolving door: they move quickly in and quickly out. That is why we have written this survival manual. We want to greatly reduce the number of athletes who flunk out of college.

Students who have difficulty in their courses generally belong in one of three groups: (1) those who have the ability to succeed but do not care about academics, (2) those who have the ability and want to succeed but do not know how to study effectively, and (3) those who have learning disabilities and are not able to do well in college courses. Because most student-athletes are in the first two groups, they can be helped by reading this book and applying its concepts and recommendations. If a student is deficient in basic educational skills—reading, writing and mathematics, he or she should seek competent remedial instruction. This book will not compensate for those deficiencies.

All of the survival skills that we suggest are applicable to both high school students and college students. Reading this book will not make athletes smarter, but it can help them to become better students. Of course, exceptionally good high school students may be able to get satisfactory college grades without fully applying themselves. But they probably would get better grades if they managed their time properly, had good study skills, and were familiar with their school's resources. The sooner an athlete learns these things, the better student he or she will become.

Below-average students can compensate for their lack of raw academic talent by putting forth extra time and effort. The best students do not always get the highest grades, but the best prepared students usually do. Numerous marginal students have proven that they can compete successfully in the classroom. Similar to excelling in sports, students who excel in academics do not always enjoy studying. Most of them would rather do something less mentally draining. What works for one person may not work for another because students vary in terms of their academic ability as well as their attitudes and habits. Becoming a successful college student is similar to becoming a successful athlete—it requires interest, ability, practice, patience, and good coaches.

There are three basic characteristics of athletes who succeed academically. First, they exhibit a high level of energy and the willingness to study even when tempted to quit. Second, they seem to have an unrelenting drive to improve their ability to make notes, read books, take tests, and write papers. Third, they have adequate mental and physical health. Student-athletes who achieve academic success often do so in spite of their sports and not because of them. These young men and women are subjected to the additional pressures of being required to (1) be at practice daily at a scheduled time, (2) study and memorize athletic-related information, and (3) travel with their teams off campus on a regular basis.

This book contains tips and techniques that can make the transition between sports and academics smoother and less stressful for most students. Nothing will make college an easy transition for all student-athletes. There are no magic formulas or copyrighted secrets in this book that will guarantee academic success. However, there is an abundance of useful, common sense, and practical tips. In the end, the techniques and tips we present are helpful only if students are willing to apply them.

Although this book is written for student-athletes, we believe that other students, coaches, teachers, counselors, parents, and librarians will find it a valuable reference guide. If only one student is able to select a suitable college for himself or herself and successfully compete academically as a result of information he or she learns by reading this book, we will have achieved our goal. This, then, is a book to be used by student-athletes and other persons to help make college a socially enjoyable and an academically successful experience.

G. H.
J. C. W.

CONTENTS

COLLEGE SURVIVAL
FOR STUDENT-ATHLETES

Chapter 1

HIGH SCHOOL PREPARATION

According to national statistics, almost 5 million young men and women participate in organized athletics in the high schools of America. The number who participate in some of the more common sports is shown below in Table 1-1, in addition to those who participate in other sports such as rodeo and lacrosse, which are generally more restricted to specific parts of the country.

But, regardless of the sport or sports in which you've chosen to compete, what you've probably already learned is that as a high school athlete, you've had to learn to accept two separate, sometimes competing, sets of responsibilities. You've had to learn how to arrange your class schedule so that there is adequate time for practice, you've had to learn how to study when your sport is in season and you come home from practice physically exhausted or come home so excited about a satisfying win that you're barely able to sit still, you've had to learn how to accept the fact that you can't take a job after school because the hours don't fit your schedule, you've had to learn that sometimes you have to miss other school activities you're interested in

TABLE 1-1

Male and Female High School Participants

Male Participants		Female Participants	
Football	923,780	Basketball	401,511
Basketball	514,791	Track and Field (outdoor)	355,652
Track and Field (outdoor)	475,229	Volleyball	269,049
Baseball	409,970	Softball (fast pitch)	188,801
Wrestling	254,581	Tennis	120,869
Cross Country	165,114	Cross Country	93,788
Soccer	162,504	Swimming and Diving	76,261
Tennis	126,458	Soccer	57,921
Golf	115,187	Field Hockey	51,076
Swimming and Diving	76,657	Gymnastics	45,736

3

because of conflicts with sports, and, finally, you've had to learn that without your wanting it, being an athlete has set you apart from some of your fellow students. It's not something you wanted to happen, but it did happen and you've had to learn to deal with those who think that because you're an athlete you can do anything you want in school, and those who think that because you're an athlete you can't do anything but compete in sports, those who give you too much and those you give you too little, in short, all of the problems that go along with being prejudged on the basis of what group you happen to belong to, rather than on the basis of the individual you are. In that sense, being an athlete is no different from many other aspects of life—some individuals will judge you prematurely and unfairly, and some individuals will have the good sense to wait and learn more about who and what you really are before making judgments. In addition, you've probably also learned something that's true about being an athlete that's important to remember in other aspects of your life; that the decision to take part in sports is one that has consequences that are both good and bad. For everything you've had to give up, there's something you've gained. For everything that's been put off for lack of time, there's been something provided. What you've had to learn is that you have to recognize the good parts and the bad parts of being an athlete and figure out if the good outweighs the bad. If you think it does, being an athlete has been a good decision. If you think it doesn't, being an athlete has been a bad decision. Almost nothing a person ever does in life is completely good or completely bad. It's a question of figuring out the balance and deciding if a particular decision is good or bad FOR YOU.

  In most situations in sports it's relatively easy to see how decisions are made. In other aspects of life it's not always so easy. The basketball center's decision to take the ball down low to the basket is related to size, position, etc. The guard's decision to shoot the jumpshot is related to the same factors, but appropriate to that individual. The center and the guard make different decisions in different situations as they evaluate the circumstances in relation to themselves. You wouldn't expect them to necessarily make the same decision, even when they found themselves in the same set of circumstances. In the same way and for the same reasons, you have to recognize that the decisions you make about whether or not you will go to college, whether or not you will continue to be involved in athletics, where to go to college, and what to do once you're there are all decisions to be made in the context of what is good FOR YOU. You need to be aware of the interaction between YOU and the college, YOU and the sports program, and the sports program and the college. This book is really about the process of making some of those decisions, some of the questions you should have answers to before making them, and how to think about some of the factors in those decisions. Spending the time necessary to make good decisions is to

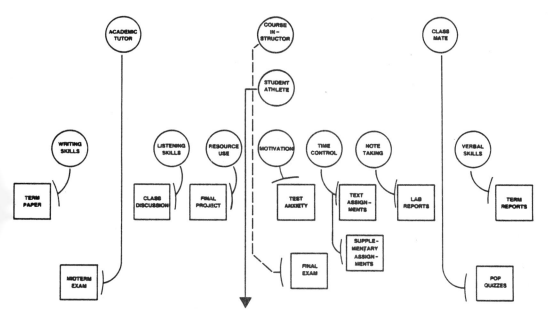

Figure 1. Academic scoring play.

your advantage because the answers to some of these questions will be critical in determining some of the directions in which your life moves in the future and in determining many of the choices and options that will be available to you.

The only person who will be able to even attempt to understand all of the inputs to these decisions—all of the emotion, all of the fears and hopes and anxieties and expectations, all of the pledges and smiles and handshakes and promises, all of the conversations and understandings and misunderstandings—is YOU. Only YOU can make these decisions and you must do so remembering that the person who will be most affected by them will be YOU. You will receive lots of advice and information from parents, teachers, friends, counselors, fellow athletes, recruiters, coaches, etc. The vast majority of the advice will be well-intended and positive, but sometimes contradictory and confusing. It is the authors' hope that reading this book will be helpful by directing your attention to some of the important questions that should be asked, and some of the factors to be considered. A two-day campus visit during which everyone is on their best behavior is pleasant, but not a sufficient substitute for your consideration of how well a particular college is likely to meet your needs for the next four years, as well as in preparing you for your adult professional life. The questions to be asked and the factors to be considered can have many answers and aspects, all of them appropriate and reasonable. Your job is to try and figure out what combination makes the most sense to YOU and serves YOUR interests best. The question of whether to go to a large school or a small school is just like the question of whether to take the ball to the basket or shoot the jumper—the answer depends on the circumstances and the context. There's no "right" answer, there's an answer that's right for YOU. While you may want to know about your teammates' decisions, and may even profit from discussing the situation with them, you have to recognize that the right decision in each person's case may differ.

If you're like most high school athletes, you probably don't even remember making a decision about becoming an athlete. Like any other child, you learned to play with your friends and as you grew older that play became more formal and regulated and focused on leagues, tournaments and competition. In any case, what you learned about yourself probably included the realization that you enjoyed play and games and competition, and that you were good at those things, which, in turn, made you enjoy them more. You may not be able to remember when you weren't involved in some kind of athletic program, in schools or summer leagues or in less organized fashion. You're one of those lucky people who have had the opportunity in your own life to understand what it means when someone uses a phrase like "the thrill of victory, the agony of defeat." That may be a bit dramatic, but if you're a high school athlete, you're a person who cares about those things. Now you're at a point in your life when you have to begin making conscious decisions about if and how to continue that important part of your life. It is the authors' belief that participation in athletics is a useful, enjoyable, productive, positive part of your life— particularly if you make good decisions about your participation. It is also the authors' belief that those decisions which give you the most latitude, that provide the greatest number of choices, that leave you in the position of selecting a particular course of action because you want to, rather than because you have to, are the best decisions for YOU. While you probably haven't thought about it in very precise fashion, you're already at the point where you have an opportunity to begin making some of those decisions that will be important to you in the future and will define your options. The first of them, and in many ways the most important since many future decisions will depend on it, is how well you prepare yourself for the academic demands of college, a decision that is critical whether you plan to continue to participate in athletics in college or not.

Far too often, students think about college preparation in terms of what is needed to get into college. The problem with that is that only half the question is addressed. What you need to be concerned with is not only what you have to do to get into college, but also what you need to do to stay in, and graduate from, college. It is important that you recognize that being a student-athlete is not, as the cynics would have you believe, a contradiction in terms. While some of you may believe that your future lies entirely in athletics, it is important to understand that while that is possible, the odds are against that happening. Even if you do eventually become a professional athlete, the average career in football or basketball lasts less than five years. So many high school athletes are awed by reading about the multi-million dollar contracts signed by superstars, no attention is paid to how few actually make it. The American Council on Education estimates that there are approximately 41,000 college football players in the country. Of these, only about 200 are drafted each year and only about 100 manage to make an NFL roster. Even with the USFL increasing the odds, you still must see what a long shot it is to plan on being one of those who will make a living in professional football. In professional basketball the same discouraging picture exists. Of 14,000 college basketball players in the country, only about 2 percent, or fewer than 300, will be drafted and only about 1 in 6 of those drafted will make an NBA roster. That means that if you are a 14 year old playing basketball and dreaming that you are the next Magic or Bird, you are having the same dream as hundreds of thousands of other 14 year olds, and only about 50 of you will make that dream a reality in about 8 years. If you are a 14 year old playing football and dreaming that you are the next Juice or Theismann, you are having the same dream as hundreds of thousands of other 14 year olds, and only about 100 of you will make that dream a reality in about 8 years. And if your dreams of fame and riches are rooted in your ability to hit a golf ball or a tennis ball, the odds are equally long. None of this should be taken to discourage you from aspiring to a career in professional sport if that is what you want. However, the point is that it simply makes sense to make decisions that recognize reality, and to conduct your life in such a way as to have other choices if that is necessary. The situation you want to be in when your college career is over, is one in which YOU are in control and in which YOU have choices. Remember that you're in very much the same situation as your friend who is in a rock band and who hopes to make it big as a professional musician, or your other friend whose talent is in science and who plans on going to medical school. All of those dreams need to be maintained, but they need to be managed in such a way as to provide other options if things don't work out as hoped. One of the things that going to college provides you with is choices—but only if you're prepared to take advantage of what college has to offer.

Preparation is critical for success in any walk of life. You know that from being an athlete. You wouldn't consider entering an important and sustained competition without adequate preparation, and that's exactly what college is. In order to compete successfully, you have to understand the level of competition and have appropriate expectations concerning your own performance. You have to learn and refine the skills required in that competition. You have to challenge yourself so that those skills grow and become more refined and stable. When you move from high school to college, you are moving from one level of competition to the next as surely as the gymnast who moves from age group to open competition. Considered from this perspective, it just makes sense for you to take advantage of whatever academic experiences your high school provides so that you can grow stronger and more competitive. Learning is a matter of application and industry, as well as native skill. "No pain—no gain" is as applicable in academics as in athletics. While you recognize that individuals may vary in ability, you also know from your athletic experience that the person who is willing to work hard and make the most of what they have will often produce more than the person who is blessed with great ability but is unwilling to work. In athletics, whether you're competing against another individual, your last performance, or the clock, it's relatively easy to judge the outcome of your efforts. In academics, judging your improvement may be more difficult, but it's no less real. Successful performance is a matter of refining skills that are built up by practice over a long period of time. Beginning skills are mastered and more difficult skills are then learned. The person who is able to compete successfully at all levels is the one who has learned the fundamentals well and built on them. The person who was a star player in a basketball league for 10 year olds because he/she was the biggest kid and never learned the fundamentals will not be a star, or even competitive, at sixteen when the other kids' growth spurts have caught up.

In considering how to use your high school experience to best prepare you for a successful college experience, remember that solid preparation will not only make you more able to compete, it will also give you more choices about areas in which to compete. The athletic analogy would be as if you were using the time before college to learn basic physical skills without choosing a sport. If you got to college having concentrated on running, balance, agility, hand-eye coordination, jumping, strength, etc., you would then be able to choose from a wide variety of sports in which to compete. In the same way, basic academic skills provide you with choices that are not available to those who haven't bothered to learn those skills. Majoring in engineering is a good example. Lots of college students today, men and women, want to consider engineering because they know that there is an attractive job market and engineers have relatively high beginning salaries. However, in order to finish an engineering degree in four years normally assumes that you will be able to start mathematics at the calculus level in your freshman year. If you have made the decision to take only the minimum number of years of mathematics required to graduate from high school, you may find yourself unprepared for the demands of an engineering major. Does this mean that you can't take courses at the college level that would prepare you for engineering? No, it doesn't. However, you can see that it makes more sense to come to college with the skills needed than to attempt to get them after you've arrived. In doing just enough to graduate from high school, or in doing just enough to be eligible for college, you may not be doing enough to be successful in college and the person being cheated is YOU.

In addition to general considerations, there are a number of practical considerations that you should be aware of in thinking about how to best prepare yourself for college. If you believe that you will be able to attend college on an athletic scholarship, you should know about some changes that are being implemented by the National Collegiate Athletic Association (NCAA). The most important change is the freshman eligibility rule which is scheduled to go into effect beginning in the fall of 1986. Under these new regulations, in order to compete at an NCAA Division I institution (those with the larger athletic programs), the student-athlete must have at least a 2.00 high school grade point average (on a 4.00 scale), and must have taken a core curriculum of at least 11 academic courses. This core must include at least three years in English, two years in mathematics, two years in social science and two years in natural science or physical science (including at least one laboratory class, if offered by the high school). In addition, the student must have at least a 15 composite score on the American College Test (ACT) or a combined score on the verbal and mathematics sections of the Scholastic Aptitude Test (SAT) of at least 700. If you will graduate from high school in 1986 or later, these regulations will apply to you.* In addition to this change in rules, the NCAA has also changed its eligibility requirements so that, beginning in 1985, a student will be required to take a minimum of 24 credits in each year (generally equal to 8 courses) *that can be counted toward a specific degree.*

It might be useful to turn our attention for a moment to why these new regulations have been enacted. Essentially, they came about after a great deal of attention was focused on what many people consider to be abuses of student-athletes at the college level. These abuses all focus on the willingness of some colleges to provide athletic scholarships to students who are unprepared for college work, to keep them eligible with courses that have no focus or collective purpose, and to abandon those students once their college eligibility is used up. There are few circumstances more tragic than that of the college athlete who has completed eligibility, who finds that a career in professional sports is not available, and who finds at the same time that the college years have been wasted in terms of a degree or any useful type of academic or professional training. Of course the student can then prepare in

---

*The NCAA is currently reviewing the freshman eligibility rule. Whether or not it is changed, it is each student-athlete's responsibility to be familiar with the rules.

earnest, but what a waste to have spent four years in a way that accomplishes so little. It's important to point out that abuses like this probably don't occur very often, but it's also important to remember that they can occur only when the student is willing to allow them to happen and when the student's preparation is such that he or she has no real choice in the matter. There's no simple way to tell under what circumstances, with what sport or coach, or at what particular college such abuses might occur. However, as in every other part of your life, the responsibility for your college experience is yours and that means you are also responsible for the earlier decisions that will largely define that experience. Providing yourself with good academic fundamentals is an important part of that experience.

Another practical consideration for you to be aware of in planning your high school career is that more and more colleges, including whole state systems, are raising their admissions requirements. This change is happening all across the country and reflects the belief that many students are graduating from high school who are just not prepared for college work. This has created a situation in which many beginning college students must spend a part of their first year taking courses that are "developmental" in nature in order to become eligible to take "regular" college courses. Where this is not required the student may find him or herself in courses for which they are unprepared and in which they have very little chance for success. In either case, it is the student who ultimately pays the price for inadequate preparation. In the newspapers or on the evening news, you have probably read or heard about lots of reports over the past few years which have been highly critical of education. The same point is made over and over again—students are leaving high school unprepared for either college or work. The increases in college admissions standards reflect that criticism and most often take the form of requiring more academic courses in order to be eligible for admission. This change is likely to remain in effect, meaning that tougher admissions requirements will be applicable to you.

Well, if you believe that adequate preparation is important, what are the kinds of abilities you should be concerned with developing to insure that you will be able to compete in the college classroom? Probably the best answer to that question is available from The College Board which began an effort in 1980 called the Educational EQuality Project. The unusual spelling of the word equality is an attempt to make clear the Board's intention that both *E*quality and *Q*uality were to be stressed in their considerations, and that this was not a retreat to an earlier era in which no attention was paid to the aspirations of minorities and the poor and the importance of education in meeting those aspirations. In 1983 the Board published a report entitled *Academic Preparation For College* in which the following statement is made:

> One of our nation's great educational triumphs is that since the middle of this century admission to college, once the privilege of a few, has been brought within

the reach of a majority of high school graduates. Yet inadequate preparation in effect deprives students of a fair chance to take advantage of this opportunity.

In recent years, many college entrants have not had the knowledge and skills needed for higher education. Many have been severely limited in their choice of college or have been unable to pursue their choice of program. Many inadequately prepared college students have dropped out in frustration or have failed their courses. Many who did graduate had such poor records that they could not go on to graduate or professional study.

What the report of the Educational EQuality Project attempted to do was bring together educators at the high school and college levels to address the question of exactly what sort of preparation high school students need to be successful in college. The recommendations of the Project are presented as "Basic Academic Competencies" and "Basic Academic Subjects."

The Basic Academic Competencies called for are defined as "... the broad intellectual skills essential to effective work in all fields of college study." These are reading, writing, speaking and listening, mathematics, reasoning, and studying. The report goes on to define the specific abilities in each of these areas as follows:

READING

- The ability to identify and comprehend the main and subordinate ideas in a written work and to summarize the ideas in one's own words.
- The ability to recognize different purposes and methods of writing, to identify a writer's point of view and tone, and to interpret a writer's meaning inferentially as well as literally.
- The ability to separate one's personal opinions and assumptions from a writer's.
- The ability to vary one's reading speed and method (survey, skim, review, question, and master) according to the type of material and one's purpose for reading.
- The ability to use the features of books and other reference materials, such as table of contents, preface, introduction, titles and subtitles, index, glossary, appendix, bibliography.
- The ability to define unfamiliar words by decoding, using contextual clues, or by using a dictionary.

WRITING

- The ability to conceive ideas about a topic for the purpose of writing.
- The ability to organize, select, and relate ideas and to outline and develop them in coherent paragraphs.

- The ability to write Standard English sentences with correct:
    - –sentence structure;
    - –verb forms;
    - –punctuation, capitalization, possessives, plural forms, and other matters of mechanics;
    - –word choice and spelling.
- The ability to vary one's writing style, including vocabulary and sentence structure, for different readers and purposes.
- The ability to improve one's own writing by restructuring, correcting errors, and rewriting.
- The ability to gather information from primary and secondary sources; to write a report using this research; to quote, paraphrase, and summarize accurately; and to cite sources properly.

SPEAKING AND LISTENING

- The ability to engage critically and constructively in the exchange of ideas, particularly during class discussions and conferences with instructors.
- The ability to answer and ask questions coherently and concisely, and to follow spoken instructions.
- The ability to identify and comprehend the main and subordinate ideas in lectures and discussions, and to report accurately what others have said.
- The ability to conceive and develop ideas about a topic for the purpose of speaking to a group; to choose and organize related ideas; to present them clearly in Standard English; and to evaluate similar presentations by others.
- The ability to vary one's own use of spoken language to suit different situations.

MATHEMATICS

- The ability to perform, with reasonable accuracy, the computations of addition, subtraction, multiplication, and division using natural numbers, fractions, decimals, and integers.
- The ability to use effectively the mathematics of:
    - –integers, fractions, and decimals;
    - –ratios, proportions, and percentages;
    - –roots and powers;

-algebra;

-geometry.

- The ability to make estimates and approximations, and to judge the reasonableness of a result.
- The ability to formulate and solve a problem in mathematical terms.
- The ability to select and use appropriate approaches and tools in solving problems (mental computation, trial and error, paper-and-pencil techniques, calculator and computer).
- The ability to use elementary concepts of probability and statistics.

REASONING

- The ability to identify and formulate problems, as well as the ability to propose and evaluate ways to solve them.
- The ability to recognize and use inductive and deductive reasoning, and to recognize fallacies in reasoning.
- The ability to draw reasonable conclusions from information found in various sources, whether written, spoken, or displayed in tables and graphs, and to defend one's conclusions rationally.
- The ability to distinguish between fact and opinion.

STUDYING

This set of abilities is different in kind from those that precede it. They are set forth here because they constitute the key abilities in learning how to learn. Successful study skills are necessary for acquiring the other five competencies as well as for achieving the desired outcomes in the Basic Academic Subjects. Students are unlikely to be efficient in any part of their work without these study skills.

- The ability to set study goals and priorities consistent with stated course objectives and one's own progress, to establish surroundings and habits conducive to learning independently or with others, and to follow a schedule that accounts for both short- and long-term projects.
- The ability to locate and use resources external to the classroom (for example, libraries, computers, interviews, and direct observation), and to incorporate knowledge from such sources into the learning process.
- The ability to develop and use general and specialized vocabularies, and to use them for reading, writing, speaking, listening, computing, and studying.

- The ability to understand and to follow customary instructions for academic work in order to recall, comprehend, analyze, summarize, and report the main ideas from reading, lectures, and other academic experiences; and to synthesize knowledge and apply it to new situations.
- The ability to prepare for various types of examinations and to devise strategies for pacing, attempting or omitting questions, thinking, writing, and editing according to the type of examination; to satisfy other assessments of learning in meeting course objectives such as laboratory performance, class participation, simulation, and students' evaluations.
- The ability to accept constructive criticism and learn from it.

The Basic Academic Subjects provide "... the detailed knowledge and skills necessary for effective work in college." These are English, the arts, mathematics, science, social studies, and foreign language. In its report for The College Board, the Educational EQuality Project discusses each of these subject areas in two ways; first, there is a presentation of why each of these subjects is important for college entrants, and second is an outline of what students need to know and be able to do in each subject area. The discussion of the individual topics students should know is too detailed to be reproduced here; however, the statement of why each subject area is important is so well-organized as to warrant its inclusion.

ENGLISH

The arts and skills of English have been at the core of college preparation for generations, and so they are today in the midst of enormous technological and social change. The skills of reading, writing, listening, and speaking will be necessary as college students are called on to read a wide variety of materials; to write essays, reports, and term papers; to express themselves aloud; and to listen to and learn from discussions and lectures. English language skills serve as the foundation for all these activities.

The technology created in today's communications revolution will be used by people, and it is the education of these individuals that commands attention. Language—written and spoken, heard and read— is central to that education. Competence in language serves a variety of purposes; accomplishing the business of daily life, communicating attitudes and ideas, expanding thought, and informing the imagination.

Because language skills are interrelated, it is not possible to isolate them in practice, even though here they are outlined separately. Moreover, while this statement includes outcomes in reading, writing, and speaking and listening as part of the study of English, it is evident that such abilities are important to and should be developed in every subject.

Although literature, language, and composition may be the special province of English, competence in writing, for example, pertains to all academic disciplines. Thus, skill in writing should be developed in other subjects as well as in English.

THE ARTS

The arts—visual arts, theater, music, and dance—challenge and extend human experience. They provide means of expression that go beyond ordinary speaking and writing. They can express intimate thoughts and feelings. They are a unique record of diverse cultures and how these cultures have developed over time. They provide distinctive ways of understanding human beings and nature. The arts are creative modes by which all people can enrich their lives both by self-expression and response to the expressions of others.

Works of arts often involve subtle meanings and complex systems of expression. Fully appreciating such works requires the careful reasoning and sustained study that lead to informed insight. Moreover, just as thorough understanding of science requires laboratory or field work, so fully understanding the arts involves first-hand work in them.

Preparation in the arts will be valuable to college entrants whatever their intended field of study. The actual practice of the arts can engage the imagination, foster flexible ways of thinking, develop disciplined effort, and build self-confidence. Appreciation of the arts is integral to the understanding of other cultures sought in the study of history, foreign language, and social sciences. Preparation in the arts will also enable college students to engage in and profit from advanced study, perform-ance, and studio work in the arts. For some, such college-level work will lead to careers in the arts. For many others, it will permanently enhance the quality of their lives, whether they continue artistic activity as an avocation or appreciation of the arts as observers and members of audiences.

MATHEMATICS

All people need some knowledge of mathematics to function well in today's society. Mathematics is an indispensable language of science and technology, as well as business and finance. All people, therefore, need some fluency in this language if they are to contribute to and fare well in our contemporary world.

More than at any time in the past the knowledge and appreciation of mathematics is essential to students' intellectual development. The advances of recent years in computer science and other highly technical fields such as space science have opened new horizons to those trained in mathematics. Young people who avail themselves of the opportunity to gain strong preparation in mathematics and in the sciences not only will grow intellectually but also keep open the door to a wide range of career choices.

Students going to college need mathematical skills beyond the elementary ones. They need a knowledge of computing to deal with the new age of computers and information systems. They need a knowledge of algebra, geometry, and functions to major in a wide range of fields, from archaeology to zoology. They need a knowledge of statistics for such fields as business, psychology, and economics.

More extensive knowledge and skills, including preparation for calculus, will be needed by college entrants who expect to take advanced mathematics courses or to major in such fields as engineering, economics, premedicine, computer science, or the natural sciences.

SCIENCE

Science—the study of the natural world—is both useful and rewarding in its own right. It provides a sense of the order in the universe and is one of civilization's major intellectual achievements. It is fueled by the same creativity required for art, music, or literature. It relies on curiosity, objectivity, and healthy skepticism. The study of science, then, is excellent preparation for college regardless of students' intended field of concentration.

Technology, which grows out of scientific discovery, has changed and will continue to change the world in which we live. Our society relies more and more on complex technology. Today's industry, agriculture, business, and professions require people trained in science and technology.

Scientific and technological developments have resulted in complex social issues that must be intelligently addressed. Such developments include: nuclear power, genetic engineering, fertilizers and pesticides, robotics, information and data processing, and organ transplantation. An evaluation of the benefits and risks inherent in these developments requires a knowledge and understanding of science and its methods.

College-bound students will need sufficient scientific knowledge to be aware of themselves as biological organisms in a physical world, to take advantage of career options requiring study of science, and to function effectively as responsible citizens in a society increasingly shaped by science and technology. They will need not only to know about science but also to understand the fundamentals of how to carry out scientific work.

SOCIAL STUDIES

The social studies focus on the complexity of our social environment. The subject combines the study of history and the social sciences and promotes skills in citizenship.

We live in a distinct kind of society and all people need to understand how such modern societies function and how they have developed. They need information concerning past civilizations and their links to present ones.

If people are to perform effectively as citizens in a democratic society, they need knowledge about central institutions and values in their own society and in other major societies around the world. They need to understand the international context of contemporary life. Defining problems and employing various kinds of information in seeking solutions to those problems require the analytical skills developed in the study of history and the social sciences.

Preparation in social studies will be important to college entrants in other ways. It will help them understand major and exciting discoveries about human beings and their social environment as well as the practical results of these discoveries. It will help them understand the context for the arts and sciences. It will help them prepare for advanced work in history and the social sciences, including anthropology, economics, geography, political science, psychology, and sociology.

FOREIGN LANGUAGE

Knowledge of another language fosters greater awareness of cultural diversity among the peoples of the world. Individuals who have foreign language skills can appreciate more readily other peoples' values and ways of life. Knowledge of a foreign language serves two other important purposes: it permits informal communication and it facilitates the exchange of ideas and information in such areas as commerce, diplomacy, science, technology, law, and the arts.

By learning another language people gain greater insight into the workings of their native language. They also can come to realize that the patterns of their native language are only one way of viewing the world. They learn how to interpret experience in other ways and to understand the close connection between language and thought.

We live in a multicultural nation. Many people speak a home language other than English. Some of these people seek to improve their proficiency in that other language and to preserve their cultural heritage. In doing so they preserve and develop a valuable national resource.

The classical languages and their literatures show the pervasive influence of Greek and Roman cultures on social and political institutions throughout Western history. Many of the words of English, Spanish, and the other major Western languages are derived from Latin. Besides such derivatives, actual words and phrases from the classical languages are present in English, particularly in law and medicine.

College entrants need a background in another language to engage in advanced study in such fields as languages, literature, and history. Knowledge of a foreign language helps students prepare for careers in commerce, international relations, law, science, and the arts.

As you read through the competencies and the subjects, you can readily see that they represent a rather broad range of abilities. Since its publication this report has been widely circulated and has been the basis for a great deal of discussion in education. Many of the recommendations have been adopted in almost exactly the form presented by the Educational EQuality Project. For example, the Education Commission of the States, in a report entitled *Action For Excellence* quotes almost exactly from the Project in a report emphasizing what it calls "education for economic growth," not just preparation for college. This underlines the importance of these competencies for all high school students, not just for those planning on going to college.

A final practical consideration of which you should be aware are the changes that are taking place in some states as they pertain to college admission. In Texas, for example, the Coordinating Board of the Texas College and University System has published a booklet entitled *Goals For College Success* in which it addresses students planning to attend college in the Texas system of higher education. The Texas Commissioner of Higher Education urges students to

> ...take four years of English and four years of mathematics. You should also take at least three years of science, three years of social studies, and two years of foreign language. You may have heard that you can get into some colleges without this much preparation. That's true. But it won't guarantee that you will be ready to face college-level work or that you will be eligible to major in the field of study you want.

After discussing the attitudes and skills which the Texas Coordinating Board considers fundamental to success in college, which they group under the headings of general preparation, communication, mathematics, reasoning, and study skills, the concluding advice given to high school students is "Your future is in your own hands. Take responsibility for it, *now*."

The Louisiana Board of Regents, in a booklet entitled *Preparing The High School Student For College,* goes further than providing general information and defines what it calls "the college preparatory curriculum" as follows:

English	4 units
English I, II, III, IV (no substitutions)	
Mathematics	3 units
Algebra I, Algebra II, and Geometry or an advanced mathematics course with geometry as a major content area	
Science	3 units
Biology, Chemistry and Earth Science or Physics	
Social Studies	3 units
United States History, World History and Civics	
Fine Arts Survey	1 unit
Students may substitute any two units of credit in band, orchestra, choir, dance, art, or drama	
Foreign Language	3 units
(in same language)	
Free Enterprise	½ unit
Physical Education	2 units
Electives or Remedial Courses	4½ units
(as necessary)	
TOTAL	24 units

This is a relatively precise set of recommendations, but one which rather fairly represents the thinking of most state systems in considering what students should study in high school in order to prepare adequately for college. Whether a state task force chooses to make its recommendations general or specific, recommended or required, the conclusion is the same:

greater preparation will be expected of the student planning on going to college. For the prospective college student-athlete who will have to satisfy the requirements of athletic as well as academic life, the message is even more urgent than for the student who will be able to devote all of his or her time and energy to the student role: prepare yourself as fully and well as possible, begin as early as possible, take advantage of as many academic opportunities as possible, and utilize the resources available to you so that you will be in a position to benefit as much as possible. A statement in the catalog of the University of Oklahoma may help make the point:

> In February of 1675, Sir Isaac Newton wrote to Robert Hooke: "If I have seen further (than you and Descartes) it is by standing on the shoulder of Giants." The point Sir Isaac was making is that knowledge in a particular area of inquiry is incremental—that it is added to and builds upon a base that has been established by prior knowledge and effort. The same point is true in regard to the knowledge that is accumulated by you as an individual—it is incremental and built upon a base which has been established by your prior efforts. In high school you begin making academic decisions which determine how solid a base you will have to build upon in college.

Chapter 2

SELECTING THE RIGHT COLLEGE

Choosing where to go to college, assuming you have decided that you will go to college, is a much more difficult decision than most people initially think. If you have gone to public schools to this point, your choice of school has generally been determined by your address or, in some relatively unusual cases, by a particular course available only in a specified "magnet" school. If you have gone to a private school, it is likely that a large percentage of the choice was determined by immediate availability and by your parents. Now that it's time to choose a college, and everyone believes that this is a rite of passage that signals your movement into adult status in our complex society, the decision is not only considerably more complicated, it's also a decision that rests far more firmly on your own shoulders.

Perhaps the most important thing to remember in looking at the more than 3,200 colleges and universities in the United States today and attempting to determine which to attend, is that the decision is, and should be, a highly personalized one. The decision as to what constitutes an appropriate choice for you is one that only you can make, although you certainly won't lack for advice and opinions from teachers, advisers, parents, friends, brothers and sisters and, perhaps more persuasively than anyone, college recruiters. The perspective you must develop in attempting to wade through all the catalogues and advice is that your job is not to attempt to rank all the colleges and universities in America, your job is to attempt to find a college or university that will be comfortable for YOU, that will provide the right academic and athletic opportunities for YOU, that will be located in an area that YOU like, that is sufficiently demanding to allow YOU to develop fully, and that places demands upon its students which are appropriate to YOU. The matter is one of fit. The question is not whether "A" is a good place, the question is whether "A" is a good place for YOU. As you develop such a perspective, you will begin to be able to sort through the boasts of particular schools with an eye to what things have real meaning to you. If you have always thought that you would like to go to a charming ivy-covered small liberal-arts college nestled in a picturesque valley in New England, it's unlikely that a sprawling, urban campus located immediately next to the business district will prove to be a good fit. If you know that you've always been interested in being an architect, the first thing you should be concerned with is whether a school attempting to recruit you has an architecture program. If immediate access to your family is one of those things that is personally important to you, don't let anyone attempt to talk you out of that feeling. On the other hand, if you've grown up in one area or neighborhood and always looked forward to moving away to go to college, pay attention to that feeling.

In spite of everyone's good intentions and desire to be helpful, you're really the only one who can even attempt to sort out all the desires, anxieties, aspirations and concerns that go into making a decision as to where to go to college. As you're probably fully aware, even you are likely to be confused by the conflicting information and feelings that have to be sorted out. However, you're the only one with any real opportunity to make sense out of it all, and you're the one who will be most affected by the decision. In many ways, the decision of where to go to college is among the most critically important that you will ever make because it establishes so many of the possibilities for your adult life. What you will major in and what sort of professional opportunities will be available will be largely determined by the college you choose to attend, many of your future business contacts will be people with whom you attended college, many of your long-term adult friends will be people you will meet in college, and even your spouse is likely to be someone you meet in college.

The purpose of this chapter is to provide you with a framework within which you can make this important judgment by insuring that you ask the right questions and pay attention to the important elements. In this, as in most other decisions in life, it is important to remember that there are tradeoffs. It is not likely that one school will be perfect in every respect. What is likely is that many choices will quickly seem unacceptable for a variety of reasons, but the remaining few choices will be difficult to choose between. Again, if you remember that an appropriate choice is a personally-dictated choice, you will find the process easier. Table 2-1 gives you a score sheet which can be used to organize some of the more critical factors involved in your decision. There may well be other factors which you may wish to consider, but these seem adequate for our discussion.

Program Availability

In a study done on a national basis and reported in *The Journal of College Admissions,* David Erdmann reports that the most important factor influencing students' choice of college is program availability in a specific area of interest. However, that is potentially misleading if we remember that many beginning college students (or these same students when they are high school seniors and engaged in the process of selecting a college) have little idea of what they wish to study in college. In addition, it should also be remembered that often students make initial decisions about majors that are based on incorrect or inadequate information.

Also, the relative popularity of some majors is often more influenced by market and other "external" factors than "internal" or personal factors directly related to the student. The current large number of students enrolled in engineering programs is an example of the effect of market

TABLE 2-1

Selecting the Right College

Below is a list of several qualities which students generally look for in colleges. It is rare for a college to have all of the qualities listed. Nor do many students expect to find all of them when they are trying to decide which school to enroll in. In the box labeled "Importance," put two checks (√√) if a quality is *very important* to you, and put one check (√) if it is *somewhat important* to you. As you visit colleges and universities, number them 1, 2, 3, and so forth, and put an "X" in the box after each quality a school has. This check list will give you quick visual analysis of the schools. (Suggestion: Before you visit a school, ask a counselor or teacher whose opinion you respect to tell you what he or she thinks are valid indications that the various qualities are present.)

Quality	Importance	College			
		No. 1	No. 2	No. 3	No. 4
Program Availability					
Academic Reputation					
Good Instructional Staff					
Good Academic Advisors					
Good Athletic Programs					
Good Dorm Facilities					
Good Eating Facilities					
Good Student Body					
Exra-curricular Opportunities					
Attractive Campus					
Good Size for a College					
Short Distance from Home					
Religious Resources					
Graduation Rates					
Scholarship Support					
Personal Items of Interest					

factors on beginning major choice. Regardless, if you know, or think you know, what you are interested in majoring in, availability of that particular program will generally be the most important single consideration in choice of college. If you are being actively recruited, don't be influenced by a recruiter's statement that a program available at the college he or she represents is "just like" the one in which you are interested. If you know that you are interested in studying marine biology in preparation for going to graduate school, don't listen to the argument that another major is really the same. Remember, it's not a question of whether the alternative major is good or not, it's a question of whether it's good for you. If you are being recruited by a representative of the athletic department, you should generally indicate your interest in talking to a representative of the academic area in which you're interested in majoring, if you're going to make a campus visit—and you should make a campus visit. It is simply logical, and appropriate, that a member of the coaching staff or the athletic department recruiting coordinator will not know all there is to know about academic programs and you must remember that it is your responsibility to insure that the information available to you is adequate to allow you to choose wisely. While it is certainly appropriate for you to keep an open mind about a particular major, if you really feel confident about that choice, stick with it and find a school that offers what you want to study.

For many of you reading this, the question of what to study is not something you've spent a lot of time on, and you're really quite undecided as to major. That's also quite reasonable, but you might also want to find out what the college recruiting you does with undecided students. Are there special processes designed to help you with that decision? Is there a "general education" or "core" curriculum that is the same for everyone in the first year or two so that the decision as to major can be deferred? Are there advisers who are experienced in working with students who are not decided? Remember that on many campuses some majors are set in a rather precise fashion so that the student who does not begin in that area will often find that that choice of major is essentially closed unless s/he is willing to spend extra time in going back and taking the proper courses in sequence. This is generally more true in professional areas such as engineering and architecture than in the liberal arts and sciences. Finally, if you are undecided as to a specific major, you should certainly pay attention as to what is available on a particular campus and determine which, if any, of those choices might be attractive. If the answer is none, you should probably not consider that particular school as a likely choice.

Academic Reputation

In the same study, the factor which students considered the second most important was the academic reputation of the school. This certainly seems most reasonable and you should certainly pay attention to this matter. However, a number of points should be raised in regard to this matter. First, find out if you can determine on what basis the particular school's reputation is based. If research productivity of the faculty is the criterion, you may wish to ask some questions about the degree to which these faculty members are engaged in undergraduate teaching. An excellent mechanism might be to see if you can simply sit in on an ongoing class or two, attempt to talk to some of the students in the class and gauge their feelings about their instruction. Every college and university will have some faculty members who are simply outstanding and some few who are perhaps less than exciting, but the overall academic reputation of the institution which eventually confers a degree upon you also confers its prestige—or lack of prestige—upon you. This may not seem important at this moment, but it may have a great deal to do with your ability to enter the graduate or professional school of your choice if that is your eventual goal. In considering the academic reputation of a particular college or university, remember that in the same sense that you help to define your own goals and outcomes by the quality of athletic competition you choose, you also help to define your own goals and outcomes by the quality of academic competition you choose. Great swimmers tend to train together and compete together in a manner that improves each individual's performance. The same is true for academic performance. It will be almost impossible for you to achieve your academic potential if you elect a less than rigorous level of competition.

Instructional Staff

While the observation has been made that the overall reputation of an institution is not necessarily the same as its teaching reputation, the important thing to attempt to determine is the importance the institution places on teaching and teaching-related activities. Again, currently enrolled students may be your best guide in this respect. Remember that it is important to define with precision what you want to know from a student about teaching in general or a specific teacher. A student may interpret "good" in regard to a teacher as an easy grader, while you may intend "good" to mean rigorous in providing a base of knowledge to be used in preparation for more advanced courses in the same area. At almost every juncture there will be decisions to be made about what courses and teachers to take and the net effect of more rigorous choices will be markedly different from less rigorous choices. It may also be helpful to remember that in most cases, reputations are of a rather diverse and general nature and you will usually have enough latitude to insure a good instructional experience, if you want it.

Academic Advising

This is an area relatively few students pay much attention to when attempting to evaluate the suitability of a particular institution, but one that almost any graduate will tell you was of great importance to the smoothness with which his/her undergraduate program proceeded. Academic advising is increasingly receiving attention in many colleges and universities, particularly at the beginning stages since this is often when many basic decisions are made and the student is the least experienced in decision-making. As an athlete, you may have access to a person within the athletic department who is specifically concerned with academic advising. However, it is important for you to recognize that you must always assume the responsibility for your program of study and the speed with which you make progress toward a degree. There are instances in which the athletic department's academic adviser may establish a schedule that allows sufficient practice time as his/her highest priority, whereas your highest priority may be in insuring that you are able to fit in the laboratory section of a course which is only offered once every two years and which is required for your major. What to do in a situation like this will, of course, depend very much upon the individual student, the institution, the specific circumstances, etc. However, the critical thing is attempting to understand what is the highest priority on the part of the institution, and how well that matches your own sense of priorities. In addition, as a prospective college student-athlete you may have some strong feelings as to whether or not you wish to be advised by a person employed by the athletic department. As we will discuss more fully in considering housing, institutions will vary greatly in the degree to which student-athletes are separated from other students. As with many other such considerations, the important thing is not the authors' value judgment as to whether this is good or bad, but your own feelings about the matter and the circumstances in which you think your best interests will be served.

Athletic Programs

If it is your hope to be a college student-athlete, it is obvious that the athletic reputation of a particular school will be of critical importance in determining its appeal to you. If you are being highly recruited as a student-athlete, you must again bear in mind that the highest-level competition, particularly in revenue-producing sports such as football and basketball, generally is accompanied by the highest level of demand on you as a program participant. If you believe that you have the ability to move from a collegiate career to a professional career, then you should attempt to follow that path. However, the odds against you are enormous and not taking advantage of the opportunities college offers in other career and professional paths is a terrible waste. Remember that while it is true that certain schools may have sent more players on to the professional ranks than others, it is also true that stars as well as journeymen players have come from every level and type of college in the country. While the overall reputation of a particular school in your sport may be important, it is ultimately the people with whom you will be associated who will determine much of your athletic success, as well as your overall degree of satisfaction with the institution. A famous coach with little or no time for you as an individual is very much like a Nobel Prize-winning teacher with little time for you with one very important difference—the coach is more intimately involved in matters that determine your success as an athlete than any one teacher would normally be in determining your success as a student.

If you are being recruited and are visiting the campus, be sure that some portion of your time is spent with athletes now on the team. Be sure that some of your time with those athletes is directed toward answering those questions in which you are interested, not just in having a good time. While college often is thought of as among the best times in a person's life, it is not all parties and fun. The support that is available to you from those most intimately concerned with you—your fellow athletes and your coaches— will be critical in determining how well you handle those stressful situations that come to all students in the course of their academic careers. The most important thing is to attempt to judge how much concern there is for you as a person, not just as a high jumper or third baseman or spiker. Even if you were to eventually have a professional career in athletics, it is your basic human values that most fully define who and what you are, and it is those values to which your coaches and fellow athletes must relate if you are not to end your college career feeling used.

Dormitory Facilities

The attractiveness of a particular dormitory is something each potential student-athlete can judge for him/herself. However, there is a question that should be addressed in a personal way that will have a great bearing on your college career: do you want to live in an athletic dormitory? As with any other such consideration, there are positive and negative points to be thought about before deciding. The important thing is to decide what is best for you. First, you might want to find out if you have any choice in the matter. If you'd like to live in an athletic dorm and a school you're considering doesn't have one, it's easy enough to dismiss that school from your list of possibilities. If a school you're considering does have an athletic dormitory, it may be necessary for you, if you become a scholarship athlete, to live in the dormitory. In many schools, particularly in non-revenue-producing sports (often referred to, wrongly, as "minor" sports), scholarships are sometimes given for portions of a student's expenses such as tuition, with no room and board and no particular obligation to live in an athletic dormitory. However, the most important single thing for you to consider is whether or not you want to find yourself in a living situation that requires you to live only with other athletes. In many ways, there is a great deal of attractiveness in such a situation; the ability to live and associate with other students who understand from their own experience what it means to be involved with a heavy practice schedule, who know how your feelings can be affected by how well or poorly a competitive situation went, who understand the kinds of sacrifices that are sometimes required to pursue a goal in athletics, and the overall sense of shared goals and purpose.

On the other hand, you may wish to consider whether or not you want to limit your circle of daily acquaintances to other athletes. After all, for most of us college is the only time in our lives when we are not actively self-segregated on some basis such as home address, level of income, professional association, etc. The college environment offers us the opportunity to meet new people who do not have backgrounds just like our own. While each and every new experience may not be attractive and enjoyable, it is the process of learning and opening oneself to new experiences that is really most important. In general, the authors believe that allowing yourself to interact on a daily basis with the widest possible variety of types of people is inherently a good thing and the most appropriate way in which to interact while in college. Of course, it can be argued that the advantages of athletic dormitories outweigh the disadvantages. The critical thing is for you to retain the final determination as to which you think will work best for you. The argument that a prospective student-athlete should probably not accept at face value is that having an athletic dormitory is essential for success in athletics, since many examples exist which demonstrate that this is simply not the case. A primary advantage of having an athletic dormitory is that it will save the athletic department money if room and board is part of the scholarship support being provided for the student. The reason for this is that the athletic department generally owns the dormitory, sometimes having built it with money donated by supporters, and housing athletes in such a dormitory is much less expensive than paying regular dormitory rates.

Eating Facilities

In attempting to judge the kind, quality and quantity of food that will be available to you, speaking to currently enrolled student-athletes will again probably be the best mechanism for you to obtain helpful information.

You may wish to determine if you are served differently during your practice and playing seasons than at other times of the year. If so, find out who is responsible for your food and if the quality changes drastically. A system that takes care of you at a different level during your season than when you are out of season, is a system that appears to value you more highly as an athlete contributing to a program than as a student concerned with his or her year-round progress and obligations. It might also be mentioned that one of the arguments used in favor of athletic dormitories is that it provides an easier mechanism for offering a training table food program for an institution's athletes than having athletes dispersed throughout the "regular" dormitories. While this argument may be true under certain circumstances, it is also true that it is not necessary to have an athletic dormitory in order to have a training table. In any case, when attempting to evaluate this particular aspect of an institution, remember that eating in any environment away from home will typically have some aspects that you may find less than wholly desirable. One of the things that beginning college students invariably express dissatisfaction with is the food in the dormitories, and this generally seems more to reflect the fact that for most new students it is the first time that they are away from home on a continuing basis, and the first time that they are unable to specify certain foods for their meals. Eating new foods can be as much of a learning experience, and as pleasant and satisfying a learning experience, as any other kind of learning, if you approach it that way. However, if you begin with the assumption that the only kind of food that is even acceptable is whatever few foods you have grown up with, you are constructing a situation in which you are almost guaranteed to be unhappy. If, on the other hand, you are open to new things—foods, ideas, people—you will be almost guaranteed a happy as well as rewarding experience.

Student Body

This is a factor that in many ways may have more to do with your happiness at a particular institution than almost any other. Regardless of your devotion as an athlete, regardless of your devotion as a student, most college-age students spend the vast majority of their time with their fellow students, receive a great portion of their personal support from their fellow students, look to their fellow students for their social activities, and simply spend the overwhelming majority of their time with their fellow students. Therefore, if you find yourself in an environment in which you perceive everyone to be of a certain "type," and believe yourself to be either incompatible or uncomfortable with that type of student, it will be extremely difficult for you to achieve a comfortable living environment. Obviously the first thing to do in examining this dimension of an institution is to simply walk around the campus and see what the people look like. Remember to just simply absorb the impressions that a walk provides you, rather than coming to any particular conclusions based on such a sketchy introduction to the campus. If the opportunity presents itself, and if you're comfortable doing so, you might want to simply stop and talk to some of the students you see and ask them their impressions of the campus while forming your own impressions of the students.

A campus visit should also provide you with information about the background of the undergraduate students, where they come from, what kinds of high schools they attended, what areas most students major in, what the mean (average) ACT or SAT test scores are, etc. Every student is always in competition with other students and is always evaluated as compared with other students. Therefore, the level of competition and the general expectation regarding academic performance, both of which are determined by the student body in general, will be important factors in the evaluation of your performance. While geography will be a factor in this decision, we will pay attention to that in considering the location of the college or university. However, it's important to remember that diversity is inherently a good thing because it provides you not only with new experiences, but with choices that may not have been available before. If you begin your college career with the belief that the only things in which you're interested are the things with which you're already familiar, you will be wasting the single most important learning opportunity of your life. College is not a time to throw away all of your past learnings any more than it is a time to reject everything that is new or unfamiliar. Your growth as a human being, in your years in college as well as throughout your entire life, will largely be a function of your ability to be open to new ideas, to take those things that are new and which might have value for you and integrate them into your life, while discarding those things which are no longer useful. Remember that neither sameness or difference is always good, and the responsibility for determining what is appropriate for your particular life style always rests with you.

Extra-curricular Opportunity

While it is true that as a person concerned with both academic and athletic obligations you will have a great deal of your time already allocated, it is also true that there will be time left unaccounted for, and extra-curricular activities will be of great importance to you as they are to all other students. One of the most important and useful lessons a freshman student typically learns is that he or she will be unable to participate in all of the activities that are a part of a typical campus and which sound so interesting. In some cases you may have been able to participate in a great variety of activities in high school including athletics, band, student government, etc. The time required to find out about all of those activities, much less participate in them, is much greater in college. In addition, many college and university environments will also provide you with the opportunity to passively participate in a number of new activities as a spectator. The art museum, plays, lectures, concerts, speakers, seminars and the increased responsibility for your educational life are all things that will have to be integrated into your patterns of living. Being a participant in everything is simply not a possibility and choices have to be made between things that may initially look equally attractive. If you are interested in a particular profession upon graduation, an active club which invites professionals in that area to campus to speak may be an important consideration. You may have a particular hobby which you would like an opportunity to continue, such as playing a musical instrument. In such a case having a band or orchestra for which students can audition would be an important consideration. Participation in student government may be something in which you are interested, or a chess club or a diving club or watching movies made in the 1930s. In any case, college should be a time for more than just the demands of school and a sport, and the broader the base of extra-curricular activities, the more opportunity you will have to participate in activities in which you are already interested or to develop new interests.

Attractive Campus

This is something that only you can judge. You may have a preference for ivy-covered tudor halls or for starkly modern high-rise buildings. In any case, this is another aspect of the general environment which will contribute to your overall feelings of happiness or unhappiness on a particular campus. While we don't feel that anyone can really tell you what to look for in judging the attractiveness of a campus, we would also remind you that the physical surroundings of the institution should be of relatively low priority in determining where you should go to school. There are far too many instances of students choosing a college on the basis of its physical appeal, only to learn to their sorrow that they didn't pay sufficient attention to the matters of programs and people, the primary determinants of the worth of their experience.

Size

Size is an interesting variable that really should be considered when looking at an individual institution. The thing to remember again is the matter of trade-offs. Both large and small institutions have advantages and disadvantages which are inherent in their size. The critical question is how much value you place on the relative pluses and minuses. Remember when you are being recruited that different types of institutions will be interested in telling you only about their best features and that you have to ask the right questions to get the full story. A small college may very well offer the warm, intimate, nurturing environment you are seeking. On the other hand, it may be restricted as to possible majors, particularly in professional areas if it is limited to liberal arts areas of study. A large state university can provide you with an enormous number of choices regarding fields of study, but if the personalized help isn't available to help you in making intelligent choices, the variety may be more confusing than helpful. The point, again, is that the important thing is how well the institution fits your needs, as opposed to whether it is "good" in some generalized sense.

The other observation that should be made regarding size is that it is probably of little meaning beyond a certain point. The question, of course, is where that point is for you. While one can readily see that a 40,000 student state university is very different from a 500 student liberal arts college, it is much less clear that an institution of 20,000 is very much different from one of 30,000, if their goals, organization, student body, etc. are comparable. The size of an institution is comparable to the size of an individual class in terms of its meaning: beyond a certain size you are simply less likely to ask questions. The class size limit for one student may be 15, while for another it may be 50. Regardless of the particular number, there is no reason to suppose that you cannot learn in a large class, and many students indicate that they sometimes prefer large classes. Likewise, a small campus may be preferable for some individuals, while a large and presumably less personalized campus may be more comfortable for others.

Perhaps the most important thing to point out is that almost every college and university in the country has staff people whose jobs consist solely of helping students. However, unless the student asks for the particular kind of help needed, he or she is unlikely to receive it. In many ways, learning to ask for help is among the most difficult and most important of things to learn on a new campus. The best and most anxious-to-help staff can't be useful unless someone is aware of your needs. When you ask to speak to an academic adviser, when you tell a dormitory adviser about a personal living problem, when you raise a question in class, you are not imposing on people's time, you are allowing them to do their job. There are no "dumb" questions. It is only dumb not to get the information you need to do your job—being a student-athlete in the most successful manner possible.

Distance from Home

This is a consideration that will vary greatly from individual to individual. For some people the idea of playing for a particular college close to home may be a dream they have grown up with and find they are able to bring to reality. For others, a particular school which has a long and rich tradition in a particular sport may be the place to play. For still others, being close enough to home to allow family members an opportunity to see you compete may be the most important single factor. None of these is either "right" or "wrong;" but one may be far more right for you. Your responsibility is to determine which that is and act in accordance with that particular factor.

Religious Resources

Of all the factors to be considered in the determination of which college or university is most appropriate for you, this is probably the most personal. However, if religious affiliation and support are items that are important to you, it is not critical that you restrict your choices to church-related institutions. Most campuses are served by priests, ministers and rabbis who focus their attention on student populations. In addition, most campuses have groups and clubs which are focused on the religious interests and needs of students. These resources, along with the possibility of your becoming affiliated with a church or synagogue in the area of the college, are likely to provide you with adequate resources in this area. On the other hand, it is not necessary for you to dismiss a religiously-affiliated institution because it is not of the same religion as you. Very few colleges or universities have a student body of only one religion. However, you should make every attempt to determine if the atmosphere at a religiously-affiliated institution is such that you will be comfortable. For most people, continual attempts at conversion are potentially bothersome and you will want to insure that you are free to participate only in the religion of your choice, or no religion if that is your choice. Finally, many institutions which began as training centers for ministers of a particular faith have evolved into distinguished universities in which the emphasis on religion is not much more pervasive than would be the case at a public university. What this all means is that you should generally not eliminate schools simply on the basis of a descriptive phrase in the title, but should take the time to examine the institution and its policies fully to determine if it is a place in which you might be comfortable.

Graduation Rates

One of the things you should find out about when you visit a particular campus is the rate of graduation of both its students and its student-athletes. You should not be satisfied with vague answers like "Oh, they're about the same." Ask to see the data and attempt to find out about the areas in which student-athletes major. You will want to avoid an institution which makes a practice of shuffling athletes into certain majors because they are easy. Such a practice rests on the assumption that you are incapable of performing your student responsibilities and pays little or no attention to you after you have contributed whatever you can to the athletic program.

Another factor to be considered is whether or not student-athletes graduate in approximately the same number of years as non-athletes. If you will be spending many hours each week in practice and play, if your sport, like basketball, extends into both the fall and spring semesters, and if extensive travel time is involved, you will be unlikely to carry the number of credits to allow you to graduate in four years. However, it is also true that many non-athletes take longer than four years to graduate. The problem arises if you will need to remain an undergraduate for more than four years and are unprepared for that fact. If your circumstances allow, attending summer school may be a way to allow you to take extra hours and graduate in four years, although for many students financial considerations will not allow summer enrollment. In any case, as discussed in Chapter 1, your focus needs to be directed not only toward admission to college, but also to graduation from college. While it is certainly true that averages may not necessarily hold for you as an individual, knowing something about the graduation rates of student-athletes at an institution you are considering may give you some information about the attitudes and values of the institution itself. Finally, if the data itself is unavailable, you may wish to ask why that is the case. Remember that the likelihood of your utilizing your athletic skills to earn a living after college is very small, and your degree, or lack of it, represents the single most important factor in determining your future financial success. While you certainly want to pay attention to opportunities for you as an athlete, you must pay attention to opportunities available for you as a student. These are not necessarily in conflict and it is your responsibility to insure that you do everything to enhance your future.

Scholarship Support

This is an area in which a great deal of misunderstanding exists and one to which you must pay special attention. Remember that the National Collegiate Athletic Association limits the extent to which scholarship athletes may receive financial aid. In speaking with recruiters from various schools there may be confusion because of different ways of explaining some aspects of aid. As an example, two schools may offer the same aid package but the recruiter from school A may tell you the package is worth $20,000 while the recruiter from school B may tell you the package is woth $40,000. The difference may simply be that the tuition and room and board rates at school B are higher than at school A. You do not receive more at B than at A. In both cases you receive tuition and room and board. Therefore, the first point is to pay less attention to the matter of number of dollars and more attention to the items which are provided for you by scholarship. Second, be sure to ask about the things that are *not* covered under your scholarship, and which you will be responsible for providing. A "full" scholarship, under NCAA regulations, is limited to tuition and fees, room and board, and books. Obviously, this does not cover other necessary expenses for personal grooming, dating, etc. In evaluating a scholarship, you need to pay particular attention to what you will have to pay for and the number of dollars those things will cost. Typically, tuition and fees at private institutions are considerably higher than at public institutions. This means that their scholarship packages will be valued at more than those offered by public institutions, but not be worth any more to you.

Another thing to be sure you understand is the precise form of the financial aid you are receiving. There are, unfortunately, some people involved in the recruitment of athletes who are less than totally honest and it is often the student-athlete who winds up paying the price of the deception. Be sure that loans are not a part of the scholarship package you are being offered. While it is often appropriate for a student to borrow money to finance part or all of his or her college costs, it is certainly a shock to find yourself with thousands of dollars in debt when you have assumed the money given was in the form of scholarships, not loans. You should avoid any temptation to sign any extensive legal documents when you are on a recruiting visit. Be sure that you can obtain a copy of any agreement you are asked to sign and have it checked by an attorney or other person you know is interested in your welfare. Your high school coach may be an excellent person to discuss this with, since it is quite possible that he or she was a scholarship athlete also.

Finally, it seems appropriate to mention something that is an unhappy part of college athletics: "under the table" payments. If you are a highly recruited athlete for a sport such as basketball or football, it is certainly possible that you may be offered cash or merchandise that is not legally part of a scholarship package. Of course, the first point to be made is that this is simply dishonest and you ought to reject such offers outright. However, such offers are sometimes made in subtle ways and may be enormously attractive. The primary thing to remember is that when such circumstances come to light, the one who generally suffers most is the athlete. The school may be on probation for some period of time, the booster club may be admonished or disbanded, the coach may even have to move on, but it is the individual athlete whose career, both as an athlete and as a student, is placed in greatest jeopardy. In addition, it is important to remember that dishonest acts do not generally take place in an honest environment. If your recruiter has been dishonest in what he or she provides in your financial support, how can you be sure that he or she has not also been dishonest in talking about the role you will play in the team's fortunes, or the alignment that is intended to maximally utilize your particular talents? The answer, of course, is that you can't be sure. An athletic program in which cheating takes place is also likely to be an athletic program in which your worth as an individual is at a minimum and your support, financial and otherwise, is likely to disappear when it no longer appears you can contribute to winning. To knowingly participate in such a program is for you to declare yourself more interested in your worth as a halfback, sprinter, guard or pitcher than as a human being. To knowingly participate in such a program is to make any future claim of innocence or pleas for mercy inappropriate and impossible to credit. While it is certainly possible that you may not know every aspect of recruiting rules and regulations, it is clearly your responsibility to protect yourself and your own good name by seeking proper advice and not allowing what seems at the moment to be a "good deal" to get in the way of your good judgment.

In summary, all colleges and universities that adhere to National Collegiate Athletic Association standards provide the same basic financial assistance. The major difference between "full" scholarships, for example, is not the money but, instead, the educational value. You should select the school that offers you the best educational opportunity, which includes athletics. Carefully select your campus, professors, coaches and courses. You should thoroughly check out a school as a visitor before you check in as a student-athlete. We suggest that you get answers to as many of the following questions as possible before you pay a visit.

- Is the school fully accredited?
- Does the school offer the courses (major) you want?
- Are your grades adequate for admission?
- Does your high school counselor believe that you can handle the college curriculum?
- Is the scholarship guaranteed for four years or can the school terminate it at any time?
- If you are injured, will you be able to keep the scholarship?
- How many hours a day will you be expected to devote to athletics?
- How much will your schooling cost in addition to the scholarship?
- If you must work to earn additional money, will you receive any help in getting a job?
- Are loans any part of the package of financial aid?
- If you need them, will the athletic department pay for tutors?
- Can you afford to travel home during vacations, and can your family afford to travel to the school to see you play?
- Would you like to play for the head coach?

- Do most of the former athletes who played for this coach have their degrees?
- Does your high school coach believe that you would fit into the college's program?
- Is the school the kind of place you'd like to spend the next four or five years?
- Has anyone attempted to encourage you to accept anything you know to be illegal?
- Has the importance of your being a student and earning a degree been emphasized?

Based on the answers to the preceding questions, select the top few schools and visit them. During these visits fill in missing information and verify the information you wish to know more about. Try to be as objective as possible and keep an open mind about things with which you are not familiar. Don't forget that when you sign a letter of intent, it's for the total institution, not just the athletic department. Select a school that offers you the very best combination of factors in which you are interested, and which offers you the best opportunity to succeed as a student and as an athlete.

Finally, do not sign anything until you receive advice which you know can be depended upon, and do not sign in the midst of a recruiting visit. When you sign, be sure everything you have been led to believe is being offered is written in full detail. After you make a decision and sign with a particular school, remember that you are part of its success and give it your loyalty and best efforts.

Chapter 3

FURTHER CONSIDERATIONS:
SELECTING A MAJOR—
EXCEPTIONAL ADMISSIONS

Once you have made the decision to attend a college or university, and have made the further decision as to which particular institution to attend, you must then face the very important decision of what to major in. For many students, this is the really critical decision, yet one that is often made without systematic consideration or by simply drifting into something. When you consider the fact that your choice of major will be crucial in determining your future professional opportunities, it really seems reasonable to at least spend some time in thinking about the choices available to you, and which seem the most likely to help you meet your goals.

Perhaps the most useful beginning might be made by attempting to define those personal goals which you consider most important. In the process of doing so, be certain that you are really paying attention to your own values and desires, rather than those of people around you. Recognizing your goals is a very personal way of thinking about yourself and it is important for you to be sure that you really understand, and are comfortable with, the goals you set. If ease of finding a job after graduating is a crucial goal for you, that should be critical in your choice of major. If finding a field in which a great deal of money can be made is important to you, that should be carefully integrated into your decision-making process. You shouldn't be at all bothered by those who want to compare your goals to theirs and judge them. Goals can be arranged in a hierarchy, but only as they apply to an individual. Goals and the values that determine them are not "better" or "purer" but are simply different. What is important is that in setting goals, your goals are set so as to be appropriate and attainable for you. The real question you must answer is "What will make you happy?" As a high school student with relatively little experience in the world of work and of decision-making, that is an extremely difficult question to answer. In fact, probably the best one can ever do is find an answer that seems appropriate at a given moment, recognizing that your values and goals are likely to change throughout the course of your life. However, the fact that the question is hard to answer certainly doesn't mean that you shouldn't attempt, as well as you can, to answer it at this time in your life.

You can begin by thinking about the courses you have already had in high school and attempting to list those which have been the most interesting, and those in which you have done best. Typically these will be the same, but not always. Remember that you should not be dissuaded from an entire field of study because of one bad experience in a class. You may find that your next experience in the same area will be far more interesting and rewarding. You should also remember that some areas of study are really basic to most majors. There used to be lots of majors that didn't require any mathematics, now there are very few as more and more fields are increasingly quantified. However, your enjoyment of a particular field or a certain type of learning should be a clue as to what areas might be appropriate majors.

Another item from your experience which may be helpful is a determination of which areas of study have been least enjoyable and successful for you. Again, a single experience may not be enough for you to form a useful opinion, but an awareness of your real strengths and weaknesses is extremely valuable in directing your attention toward, or away from, particular areas. You might wish to think about the types of areas that have been both pleasant and unpleasant in such terms as were they areas in which "right" answers and problem-solving were important, such as many of the sciences, or were they areas in which imagination and the ability to be creative were most important? These are certainly not mutually exclusive, and many students can enjoy both such areas, as well as do well in both, but this is another way in which to think about various fields of study.

Think about the people you know who seem the most interesting to you; what do they do? Think about those who seem the most absorbed and interested in their work; what do they do? Think about the kinds of occupations you see shown in movies and those you read about in novels; what seems the most attractive? What are friends thinking about becoming? All of these are useful for helping you to think about various kinds of professions and jobs but are only part of what must be considered. You must think about how much time you are willing to spend in preparing for a particular career. Physicians are portrayed as glamorous and wealthy figures, but unless you are prepared to spend four years as an undergraduate, four more years in medical school and further years as a resident, you need not even consider medicine as a career. While the preparation time for being a lawyer is less, it is still approximately seven years of school. Many students initially consider a particular career field without sufficient information about the requirements for entry performance. For instance, many students speak of majoring in psychology and when pressed to fully describe what they mean, they often mean the practice of clinical psychology. That is an area which also requires academic preparation beyond the bachelor's degree and in which there is a great deal of competition for admission to graduate programs. You should also attempt to find out about fields of study which are related to those in which you have an initial interest and determine which might be more attractive or more feasible. For example, if medicine seems interesting but impossible for financial reasons, you might wish to consider nursing, medical technology, physical therapy, dentistry, pharmacy, physician's associate, radiation therapy, or any of several other health fields of which you may not even be aware at this moment.

Another factor to consider, as discussed in Chapter 1, is how quickly a particular college will require you to declare a major. If you are able to begin your college career without a declared major, that should allow you to take advantage of whatever counseling and placement services are available at your particular school. Sometimes, all a student needs to know to make a decision about a major is what career paths might be open if he or she studies a particular subject. At other times students will want to know what beginning salaries are in a particular field. Still another type of information which may be available about a field in which you are interested is what the U.S. Department of Labor predicts about the supply of jobs in that field for the next few years. Sometimes a student will begin study in a major as a freshman with the expectation that jobs will be plentiful, and in the course of the next four or five years jobs become scarce, leading to disappointment and frustration. Sometimes students are interested in fields which appear to be the least crowded at the moment, anticipating changes in the job market. Still other students have no desire to find out about the externals related to a particular area, since they "know" they wish to be a teacher or a coach or a writer or a physician or a social worker or a chemist. Whether you "know" or are just searching, it will be to your advantage to learn about the resources your career planning office provides. Even if they only provide help in writing your resume and setting up appointments with prospective employers, that will be a considerable service that is performed far more efficiently than if you had to manage on your own.

Another source of information often overlooked by students is a faculty member in a particular area you enjoy but in which you fail to see a professional future. This is most often true in social science and humanities areas in which a faculty member in an area such as sociology can tell you about the various types of work done by persons with bachelor's level degrees in sociology. You shouldn't hesitate to raise questions of this nature with faculty members, since most are so vitally interested in their particular area of study, they generally will be extremely happy, perhaps even flattered, to discuss professional opportunities with you.

Finally, you should be aware of the fact that most colleges and universities have testing programs which are sometimes useful in helping you sort through various professional and major possibilities. Generally, these are of two kinds: interest inventories and aptitude tests. The interest inventories are exactly what their name suggests—a systematic way of helping you to assess your interests, as well as information about professional opportunities which may be well-matched to those interests. The aptitude tests attempt to assess the general categories of work for which you may be suited, generally as demonstrated by your abilities. The important thing for you to remember is that it is impossible for any sort of test to provide you with extremely precise information about what might be an appropriate choice of major or profession. Such a choice is extremely difficult to make and extremely important as well.

What that means is that you must utilize whatever resources are available and appropriate to help you with making that decision. The testing programs are a part of this process but cannot be thought of as a substitute for your judgment. Tests can provide information useful in making a decision, but should not be the sole basis for a decision of this importance. The extremes that you would be wise to avoid in the process of choosing a major are simply allowing yourself to drift into a particular major because it seems convenient or easy or you are discouraged about finding a major which might be exciting, or, on the other hand, allowing your choice of major to be dictated by a mechanical testing program that cannot fully measure all of the complex and personal factors involved in such a decision.

EXCEPTIONAL ADMISSIONS

This is a topic that is directed to those of you who, to this date, have not done well in your grades, regardless of the reason. Of course, if you were to follow all of the advice in this book, these observations would not be applicable, because with almost no exceptions, sufficient study in combination with good study habits will produce learning and decent grades. However, it would be foolish not to recognize that for some individuals, because of lack of interest, lack of time, lack of concentration, poor early learning experiences, or some other factor, the time will come when you are being actively recruited as an athlete and find that you are not admissible to that particular college or university. What do you do then? Well, in many cases, colleges and universities have what are known as exceptional admissions categories. That is, they can admit a certain number of students who do not meet the regular criteria for admission. These policies are established to allow the individual institution some flexibility in regard to admissions. Usually these policies are stated in rather vague terms such as "unusual abilities that are not demonstrated on standard academic measures." The example given is almost always that of a student who possesses exceptional artistic talents but has done poorly in grades. However, the interpretation of "unusual ability" that most often is followed in practice is the ability of a 209 pound running back to cover 40 yards in under 5 seconds while carrying a football. The question for you to be concerned with if you find yourself in a situation in which you can only be admitted to a particular college as an exception is whether or not that is a place you should seriously consider. The answer, as always, is complex but one that you should pay particular attention to. On the one hand, the argument can be made that if a student has not done well on standardized tests (ACT or SAT) or on his or her previous grades, this does not necessarily mean that that same student cannot do well in college. That is true, but we are more concerned with what is likely than what is possible. The fact remains that previous learning, or lack of learning, generally has an effect on future learning. As we discussed in Chapter 1, if you are not well prepared for college, you are not likely to do well, although prior poor efforts can be overcome with enough effort. However, the point to be considered in this discussion is whether your best interests are likely to be served by attending a college whose admissions criteria you do not meet.

The best advice would seem to be to attempt to find out everything you can about the institution's policies in regard to exceptional admissions. You should ask if exceptional admission is used for students other than athletes. If it is not, that may indicate an institution which treats its student-athletes very differently from other students, typically a situation that should raise warning signals in your mind. You should attempt to find out what sorts of majors students who have been admitted as exceptions in the past have chosen. If you are not able to find out this sort of information, you may wish to ask why it is not available. Is the institution hiding something? Does the institution know but find the statistics embarrassing? Does the institution not monitor the progress of students who are admitted on probation, just getting them in and then leaving them to fend for themselves? What about the graduation rate of athletes who are admitted as exceptions to the regular admissions policies? Do they graduate at the same rate as other student-athletes? Do they graduate at the same rate as other students? Do they graduate at the same rate as other students who are admitted as exceptions? These are all extremely important questions in attempting to determine the seriousness with which a particular institution treats students who are admitted as exceptions.

As stated before, it is your responsibility to remember that there is a vast difference between getting into a particular school and graduating from that school. Every college and university that has admissions standards is actually using those standards to tell you something about your chances of being successful in its programs. If you must be admitted as an exception, you are placing yourself in a position in which you should recognize that you are fighting against the odds. While you may overcome those odds, you should recognize that they exist and that it will require extra effort on your part to be successful. At one major university in which the success of student-athletes was surveyed, it was determined that athletes who were regularly admissible graduated at approximately the same rate as other students, although it tended to take them longer to graduate, while athletes who had to be admitted as exceptions usually failed to graduate. What this reflected was a situation in which athletes were being recruited solely for their contribution to the athletic program, with little or no regard for their success as students. Remember the odds against your ever making a living as a professional athlete and remember that college, for most people, is the single best opportunity to develop the skills and earn the credentials that will allow them to be in a competitive position when it is time to enter the workforce. While it is certainly true that college, at its best, is a great deal more than simply preparation for work, it is also true, particularly in these days, that many undergraduate students are vitally concerned with job choices and view this as a primary benefit of attending college. You should keep an open mind about attending a particular college if you cannot meet its regular admissions criteria, but before making a decision be sure that you address the types of questions that are mentioned in this section. Do not allow your enthusiasm for the institution's athletic program to blind you to the realities of the demands of the academic program, and your chances for success in those programs.

Chapter 4

ADJUSTING TO COLLEGE

By the time you are finally ready to leave home for college, the thing you will have heard more than any other is "It's really going to be a change. College just isn't anything like high school and you'd better be prepared." In fact, you've probably heard that a lot already—from parents, teachers, counselors, older brothers and sisters, and from anyone else who has an opinion about your future, which probably includes everyone you know. Well, as is often the case, the reason that phrase is so common is that it has a great deal of basis in truth. On the other hand, you, knowing exactly how bright, adaptable, clever, charming, insightful, and sensitive you are, may very well be convinced that everyone is making too much of a really easy thing—going off to college. Well, you may be right in that your abilities will help you a great deal. On the other hand, it never hurts to be prepared, and in this chapter we would like to mention some of the things that might be helpful to you as you begin your college career.

The greatest single change that occurs when you move from high school to college is a shift in responsibility that generally results in the burden for decision-making to be shifted from wherever it has been up to this point—parents, coaches, teachers—to *YOU*. The reasons for this shift in responsibility are many, but probably the most important single one is that all through high school you have been regarded as less than an adult. School is required until graduation from high school, or a certain age which varies from state to state, and the general assumption is that since you are not able to make decisions about where to be and what you are doing, you are not yet an adult. All of those assumptions change at the college level and you are generally regarded as an adult. Almost any student who is asked about that change will say that they prefer being regarded as an adult, but often that comment is made without full understanding of the impact of moving to adult status, and the greatest single change is the necessity of assuming responsibility for your own life and your own decisions. This change is

44

manifested in many ways from items as mundane as sometimes having to learn how to run a clothes washer and dryer since your laundry will no longer be done as part of the family's, to far more meaningful and serious things such as what career to pursue or, even, whom to marry. What this means is that at the same time that you are being asked to assume the responsibility for the decisions that affect you, the number and type of those decisions is increasing and becoming more complex. However, rather than viewing this as a burden, you should remember that it is a necessary part of learning and growth, and, happily, this change takes place in a relatively protected environment. The possibility of causing yourself real harm in learning to make decisions would be far greater if, rather than going to college, you choose to open a business upon graduation from high school with your entire family's life savings being used to get started. After all, regardless of the particular college or university you choose to attend, there will be rules and regulations and requirements that will largely define what options are available to you in many areas. However, the range and complexity of the decisions will still be far greater than you have probably been used to, and care and caution should be part of your approach to the whole college experience. Remember that your responsibility is not just to make choices, it is to make good choices.

In general, the most important single piece of advice that new students can take to heart is "ASK QUESTIONS!" The transition from high school to college is invariably made more difficult by the fact that you move from being a senior in a high school, which typically makes you at least a bit of a hotshot, to a lowly freshman. In the case of a student-athlete, the problem is often made more difficult by the fact that in high school everyone probably knew you as a campus hero, due simply to the fact that you were involved in athletics. Now, particularly if you have chosen to be on a relatively large campus, you find yourself just one of many new students who must learn about a new place, meet new people, master new mechanical procedures, all without the familiar support mechanisms and people that you have used for the past four or more years. It's no wonder that the first few weeks are likely to be a time for anxiety in addition to excitement.

The initial reaction of many new freshmen, because they are uncomfortable and feel somewhat out of place, is to pretend that they know exactly what they are doing when they do not, and being caught asking questions is the last thing they are interested in. What often happens in circumstances like these is that students wait to find out the things they need to know until it is sometimes too late for them to have useful choices in many matters. For an athlete this is sometimes an easier time than for other students since you may have access to people in the athletic department with whom you are already familiar and with whom you will feel comfortable asking questions. However, we would again point out that it is important for you to recognize that if you fail to check information, whether it comes from your roommate or a coach, the consequences of wrong decisions will be entirely yours.

While earlier in this discussion we emphasized the increase in complexity of decisions in college, at least somewhat due to the college's size, it is also important to emphasize that this increase in size also allows every college and university to employ individuals, either in student services or academic areas, whose job consists entirely of helping students. Perhaps the way to think about the process of asking questions in a new campus environment is to recognize that without you and your fellow students seeking information, these people will be out of work. Whether your humanitarian effort is directed to yourself or to the appropriate professional personnel, asking questions is terribly important. This is no less true in your classes than in general. While large lecture classes may make it difficult to ask questions, most faculty members maintain office hours and are accessible to their students. However, it is your responsibility to see that your questions are answered, not the faculty member's responsibility to come to you and see if you need anything. When thinking about asking questions of faculty members, students are often reluctant to do so, feeling that they will be imposing. While an individual faculty member may sometimes give you that impression, what you will typically find is that most faculty members are so wrapped up in their fields, they are not only willing, but enthusiastic, about discussing their area further. You must remember that college professors are like every other group of professionals—doctors, lawyers, accountants, managers, etc.—some very few will be absolutely outstanding, some very few will be quite poor, and the vast majority will be somewhere in the middle, whether you are evaluating their ability to make their presentation interesting, or their enthusiasm for their subject. The rare faculty member who has no time for his or her students is simply an experience you will have to learn to deal with in the most effective manner possible. Don't be discouraged if it happens to be one of your first experiences, it's quite rare.

Another area with which you should become familiar as soon as possible is the academic support services which are available. Almost every college or university will offer both credit and noncredit courses in such things as reducing test anxiety, time management, effective study habits, reading improvement, test-taking, note-taking, etc. Most of these and similar topics are covered in later chapters of this book, but may be positively reinforced at the college level. In some schools, an orientation course is given to freshman students, although rarely required these days, which familiarizes the student with the procedures used on campus for adding or dropping courses, paying fees, taking advanced standing examinations, enrolling, etc. While much of the material in these courses is often of an extremely elementary nature, the typical beginning freshman student can learn a great deal from them, including how to avoid many of the mechanical problems which often cause real problems for students.

Two additional services which are sometimes available are test files and tutoring which can be exceptionally helpful. Test files have been a part of the college scene for many years, but they were typically only available when organized groups managed to put them together, thus providing an unfair advantage to students who had access to those groups. Today many campuses ask faculty members to provide extra copies of examinations which can be examined by future students as a means of preparing for examinations in classes taught by those faculty members. To the student it is a way of familiarizing him or herself with the kind of material the professor emphasizes and the kinds of questions he or she likes to ask. For the faculty member it is a way of directing the attention of the student to the material that is most important. Making such test files available to all students insures that any student who wishes can have the same advantages of preparation as any other student. Tutoring services are often provided, particularly in large institutions, in introductory-level courses in which many beginning students enroll in large sections. Very often such tutoring services are offered free of charge and can be extremely helpful in understanding particular portions of a course which prove troublesome. These and additional services are also typically described in orientation courses offered for beginning students.

Whichever college or university you attend will be likely to have some medical and counseling services available. Be sure to learn about them and take advantage of them. If you are in school in the center of a large city, the medical services provided by the college may be rather minimal, whereas the medical services on campus provided by a state university in a very small town may be as extensive as providing minor surgery and hospital care. In either case, campus medical services are usually reliable, convenient and relatively inexpensive. If you are going away to college and have particular medical problems which require periodic attention, be sure to ask your family doctor for the name of someone in the area to be referred to, and be sure that your medical records reflect your full medical history. As an athlete, you are likely to have greater access to medical care, usually including the necessity for periodic physical examinations. The periodic midwinter cold or flu that makes you feel lousy will be a barrier to your best performance, both in athletics and academics, and can be greatly alleviated by your taking advantage of the medical services your campus has to offer. Trying to find a local physician who will take you when you need to be seen if you are not a regular patient can be a frustrating experience.

Be sure that you find out about the academic counseling services which are available. Even if you are interested in a major that is rather precisely defined as to content, such as many of the engineering areas, and there is a degree checksheet available which describes the courses needed for the degree, there is always latitude regarding the sequence in which some courses are taken, the best electives considering your interests, etc. Most degree checksheets also begin with a series of assumptions concerning the academic background of the students who will major in a given field, some of which may not be appropriate in your case. An example might be a degree checksheet in a field such as civil engineering which can be followed easily, but which requires that a first semester student begin with calculus. For many students intending to major in engineering, the assumption that the student has had enough mathematics in high school to allow him or her to begin with calculus may be a good one. However, the student who simply follows the checksheet without adapting it to his or her own circumstances will find enormous difficulty in the first semester. On some campuses you will be required to see an academic adviser before being allowed to enroll. On other campuses, or in some areas of study, it may be up to you to talk with an adviser if you wish. The adviser will sometimes be a faculty member, and sometimes a person whose entire job is academic advising. In any case, it is very much to your advantage to speak with an adviser, and to do so when he or she has time to really discuss your needs and objectives. Don't wait until the day before enrollment when everyone on campus is trying to be advised. You will find that adequate planning will have substantial benefits for you in the ease with which your program proceeds. An academic adviser is not a hurdle to be overcome, he or she is a source of help, encouragement and support for you.

In the midst of all the excitement about moving into adult status, in moving to a new and exciting location, and in discovering new challenges in both the athletic and academic portions of your life, it's probably wise to mention that if you're like most every other freshman student, there will be some moments of anxiety, sadness and homesickness. For most beginning students, moving to campus is the first period of extended separation from family and friends, and it is only normal and natural to expect that there will be times when you miss the people and places which have been a part of the first 18 or so years of your life. If you know that this is possible, you're less likely to remain depressed for any extended period of time. However, if you do find yourself feeling down for a while, probably the best thing to do is talk about it with someone you like and trust. As an athlete, you again have an advantage in that one or more coaches may be available to you immediately, particularly if one or more has been involved in recruiting you to the campus. In addition, one of the causes of feeling depressed for many new students is the feeling that now, cut off from friends and family, without new support people in place yet, they are quite alone in dealing with new demands in a new place. For the student-athlete, knowing that you are a part of a team, having access to other freshman athletes to whom you have been introduced, and knowing coaches, trainers, etc. can provide an instant sense of community and belonging which are important in adjustment to college life. One of the things that you can do if you do have some down moments is simply fall back on your family. Call home in the evening when it doesn't cost very much and take advantage of the support available there. Even though, as an athlete, you're immediately part of a group, it's also true that you may immediately be placed in a competitive situation which doesn't go exactly as you hope. For the student-athlete involved in football, with freshmen eligible for varsity competition, the first few weeks of the first semester can be an extremely trying time, and you may need every source of support you can muster. While everything seems new all at once, don't forget that you've been coping with new demands and new situations all your life, and you will cope with these too.

An important person with whom you will be spending a great deal of time will be your roommate, assuming you do not have a private room on campus. For many students, this will be the first time that you will have to share, on a continuing basis, what has previously been private space. Finding a roommate with whom you can be comfortable is quite important in making the adjustment to college and depends as much on you as the other person. While you are checking him or her out carefully, the same is being done to you. Do you want to be given an adequate amount of time to be judged? So does your roommate. Remember that even if your roommate has a background very different from yours, there will be more things alike than unlike between the two of you. It may even turn out that some of the things that are different are both interesting and attractive. This is another in a series of circumstances in which proceeding with an open mind is terribly important. While newness can sometimes be somewhat unsettling, it is also exciting and interesting, no less for people than places or activities. Try to establish open communication with your roommate as soon as possible. No matter how hard both of you try, there will be things that each of you will find annoying about the other. If you can talk about those things openly and without anger before they get to be really a problem, you will have a key to living with another person, a skill that will stand you in good stead throughout your life. The same holds true for the way in which you interact with all of your new teammates and fellow students. Remain open, be honest, and retain your own sense of what is acceptable and appropriate. By the time you get to college you will typically be 18 or 19 years old and are far from unformed and without values or beliefs. While the college years are a time for trying new things, that doesn't automatically translate into rejecting all of the things you have known before. While openness is very much to your advantage, don't confuse it with being a sponge and simply taking on the values, attitudes, beliefs and behaviors of new people. Your job in this time of growth and learning is to experience new things and sort among them to find what works for you and is comfortable for you.

Another aspect of college life which you will have to consider is what number and type of activities you will choose to spend your time on, in addition to your academic and athletic activities. In college, what you will find is that the variety of extracurricular activities available will be such that choices will be necessary. For some relatively few, and extremely fortunate, individuals, high school is a time when you are able to engage in almost every activity offered. Even within large high schools, it is not totally unusual for one student to be strong academically, play varsity ball, be president of the senior class, and be in charge of homecoming. When this same individual gets to college, what he or she will almost always find is that they are no longer able to participate in everything and choices have to be made. In addition to all of the activities that were available in high school, now there is probably an array of film series, discussion groups, political groups running across the entire political spectrum, plays, dance presentations, museum exhibitions, a wide variety of activities focused on specific professional and academic interests, a much wider array of athletic activities than was available in high school, special interest groups focused on every imaginable recreational activity such as chess clubs and hang-gliding clubs and everything in between, and all of this in combination with more demands on available time for both academic and athletic performance than was previously the case. No matter how talented the individual, he or she must make choices about what things to participate in. Obviously, the first thing that should determine those choices is your interest. If you are determined to go on and earn an M.B.A. from the most prestigious institution possible, your participation in an undergraduate business students association may be a very wise use of time. If you have always been interested in theatre and want to participate in presenting plays, as an actor or in some backstage capacity, you should make every effort to make the time to do that. If you are interested in the possibility of a career in scientific research, time spent assisting a faculty member in a laboratory would be extremely useful. Regardless of the interests you may have, you are likely to find some formal or informal organization or means for engaging and expanding that interest.

There will also be other activities available on campus that you have not previously been familiar with, and you should take the opportunity to at least take an initial look at those which you might find interesting if you were to learn more about them. As an example, you may never have known much about, or cared much about, art. If the campus you attend has an art museum, and it is likely to, you might be quite pleasantly surprised to find how enjoyable a few hours spent in the museum might be. A discovery of that sort might be useful in also helping you make decisions about elective courses in which you might be interested. If you have never been interested in politics but would like to find out more about them, look into joining a local student political group, or even running for campus office. Student-athletes begin with the advantage of a great deal of campus visibility, but often do very little with that visibility, other than enjoy it. Campus politics may be an enjoyable activity, particularly as you reach voting age and are able to participate more fully in the political process. The point again is to remain open to new experiences, to explore new interests, to reinforce already existing interests, and to take advantage of being on a campus.

To an inquiring mind, a campus is like a candy store filled with various attractive and flavorful kinds of intellectual possibilities. It's impossible to have all of them, but a reasonably large number can be sampled, and should be. While most people stress that your years in college should be among the happiest and most satisfying in your life, not enough attention is given to the fact that what contributes greatly to the attractiveness of this time is the sheer excitement of being on a campus, of being in a place in which people are intellectually alive and in which your own intellect is stimulated on a constant basis, an environment in which you can pick and choose among enormously different kinds of activities for profit and gain or for sheer enjoyment; in short, a time in which you can indulge yourself and can do it in an efficient manner. In the portion of your life leading up to college, there are typically rather real limitations on your activities due to a limited number of courses, clubs, activities, etc. In the portion of your life after college, there are typically limitations due to the necessity of earning a living, of providing for the emotional and other types of support for a family, for meeting the expectations of others such as bosses, and the demands of time. While it is certainly true that many of these same limitations may exist while you are in college, it is also true that for most people the limitations will be more self-imposed than set by others, and the environment will encourage your explorations more than at any other time. If you do not take advantage of that time and opportunity, you are, quite simply, wasting an opportunity that will not come again. The one who will be cheated is you, not the institution which will have other students to look forward to.

You might also wish to consider joining any of a variety of social clubs which exist on most campuses. These are known as fraternities and sororities, eating clubs, house plans, etc. Regardless of the name, their longevity or their degree of formality, they are all voluntary organizations which offer their members an opportunity to live together in many cases, and conduct their social activities together. Of course, if you are a scholarship athlete, it may be necessary for you to live in either a college dorm or the athletic dorm in order to receive the room portion of your scholarship. If this is true, some type of affiliation is often possible, even though you do not live in the group's house. Quite often such social groups will have a history of being focused on a particular type of interest, such as intramural athletics, music, student government, etc. You should attempt to find that group which best matches and complements your interests. However, two things should be mentioned as you consider the possibility of such social organizations. First, you should make every effort to insure that the people in the group are people with whom you would like to associate on a regular basis, as well as insuring that the group is interested in you as a person, rather than as an athletic trophy they can parade around for reasons of social prestige. As an athlete you may already have experienced the type of individual who assumes that his or her social prestige is enhanced by hanging around with athletes who typically have a good deal of social prestige. Most athletes, except for those who are quite immature, find this type of relationship quite a burden and generally choose to spend their relatively rare, and therefore quite precious, free time with people who are genuinely their friends, rather than hangers-on. Of course, the real difficulty always lies in attempting to determine who is truly a friend and who is just interested in you for what you are. The second consideration in evaluating such social groups is to be sure that you will have enough time to spend with the group. You would be unwise to attempt to become part of a social organization if you simply do not have the time to be social, at least within the context of that group. Remember that many students find such social organizations useful because it provides them with a point of identity in a rather large institution which they find somewhat intimidating. If the team and athletic department provides that point of identity for you, an organization which requires more time than you have to devote, may be an unwise choice. Also remember that joining such an organization is not usually a decision that has to be made in your first semester. If you determine in your second semester or second year that you would like to join a particular social group, that possibility is usually available.

Finally, as you look ahead to making the various types of adjustments that college will require, you should also consider the basic outcome that should be derived from going to college—an education. Your response to that comment is probably "Well, of course." However, we would like to emphasize the difference between education, in its broadest and most important sense, and vocational or professional training. While it is important to recognize how interested students typically are in job possibilities after graduation, it is also important to recognize that a college degree should represent broad-based learning that not only is important for its own sake, but also prepares you for a lifetime of learning; that imbues you with the appreciation of knowledge and its application, and that provides you with the basic skills and understandings that serve as the basis for future learning. In this sense, education is a much broader and more meaningful type of learning than training which is specific to a particular task or job, and which has very little potential for application to other tasks. The elements which contribute to education in this sense we have already discussed; an understanding of yourself, your needs, abilities and background, your values, your professional goals and your ability to be open to new ideas, activities, values and attitudes while not indiscriminately discarding the old. As an athlete you have already learned the values of preparation and having a good strategy to achieve your goals. As a student, these same elements will also contribute to your success if you apply them with vigor.

Chapter 5

TIME MANAGEMENT

Do you have time to do everything you want to do? If you are like most people, the answer to this question is "no." And, also like most people, you probably are reluctant to admit that you need help in learning to effectively use your time and academic abilities. Athletes tend to be proud people who consider a need for help as a weakness. Thus, many athletes would rather fail a course than admit to other persons that they need help. But this is not limited to athletes. Few students actively seek academic help when they need it. Winning in the classroom under these conditions is a hit-or-miss activity reflecting luck instead of well-developed study skills.

If you are a moderately successful athlete, you do not leave your performance in your sport or sports to chance. On the contrary, you seek out expert help, follow a training routine, and are constructively critical about your performances. A similar effort is needed in order to be successful in the classroom. That is, you need an *academic game plan*. If you have learned to manage your time in sports, that ability will be useful in academic time management, too.

STUDY SKILLS ASSESSMENT

Developing good study skills is similar to developing good sport skills. It requires a sincere desire to learn, considerable practice, and the guidance of a competent coach. Teachers, counselors, librarians, and other school personnel are academic coaches. The academic practice and competition areas are classrooms, libraries, auditoriums, and all other places students gather. Your success as a student will depend to a great degree on your ability to organize your time and effort and utilize proven study skills techniques.

The study skills survey printed below is divided into three parts: (1)

study motivation, (2) study organization, and (3) study techniques. *Study motivation* measures how well you accept school and adjust to teacher activities and assignments. *Study organization* measures how well you use your study time and organize your study area. *Study techniques* measure your ability to read assigned material, take notes, write reports, and take tests. There are no "right" or "wrong" answers to the questions. There are only your answers. Do not spend much time on any question and answer all of them honestly. If the answer to a question is "Yes," put a check mark in the box in front of its number.

Study Motivation
☐ 1. Do you usually do only enough to get a passing grade in your courses?
☐ 2. Do you believe that academic work only takes time away from your athletic work?
☐ 3. Do you believe that having a good time outside of school is more important than studying?
☐ 4. Do you lose interest in most of your classes after a few days or weeks?
☐ 5. Do you often spend class time daydreaming or sleeping instead of listening to the teacher?
☐ 6. Are you unable to devote time to your studies because of boredom, restlessness, or lack of interest?
☐ 7. Is your study hit-or-miss depending on your moods?
☐ 8. Do you feel that the courses you have taken will not prepare you to get the job you want?
☐ 9. Do you seriously think about dropping out of school and getting a job?
☐ 10. Are you frequently confused and undecided about your educational and athletic goals?
☐ 11. Do you dislike reading textbooks because they are dull and boring?
☐ 12. Do you wait until a day or two before a test to read your assignments and review your notes?
☐ 13. Do you believe that you are taking courses that have little practical value to you?
☐ 14. Do you feel that your teachers demand too much work from you?
☐ 15. Do you usually hesitate to ask your teachers for help with difficult assignments?
☐ 16. Do most of your teachers lack understanding of the needs and interests of student-athletes?

Study Organization
☐ 1. Do you usually wait until the last minute to prepare reports?
☐ 2. Do you usually wait a day or more before reviewing your class notes?
☐ 3. Do you frequently go to class too tired or too sleepy to study effectively?

☐ 4. Do athletic activities often cause you to neglect your coursework?

☐ 5. Do you often fail to complete homework assignments on time?

☐ 6. Do you sometimes get behind in one class because you have to study for another?

☐ 7. Do you frequently spend time watching television, listening to music, reading magazines, or exchanging gossip when you should be studying?

☐ 8. Do you seem to spend a lot of time studying but accomplishing very little?

☐ 9. Do you sometimes discover that you have fallen asleep while studying?

☐ 10. Do you keep photographs, trophies, and litter on your study table or desk?

☐ 11. Does the lighting in your study area create a glare on your reading material?

☐ 12. Do visitors to your room often interrupt you when you are trying to study?

☐ 13. Do you take a lot of long breaks when you study?

☐ 14. Do you usually study with a television, stereo, or radio playing?

☐ 15. Is your studying often disturbed by people or noise outside your room?

☐ 16. Do you often find that you cannot complete your studying because the books and study materials you need are missing?

Study Techniques

☐ 1. Do you usually read course materials only before a test?

☐ 2. Do you normally begin reading a textbook assignment before surveying the unit headings and illustrations?

☐ 3. Do you get behind in your notetaking because you can't write fast enough?

☐ 4. Do you often have difficulty making sense of your notes?

☐ 5. Do you try to copy lectures word for word?

☐ 6. Do you frequently have difficulty picking out the important points in your reading assignments?

☐ 7. Do you have great difficulty selecting topics for reports?

☐ 8. Do you usually prepare term paper outlines after the reports are written?

☐ 9. Do you prepare for tests by trying to memorize definitions, rules, and formulas that you do not understand?

☐ 10. Are you confused by most multiple-choice tests?

☐ 11. Do you usually run out of time when taking essay tests?

☐ 12. Do you have difficulty organizing your study material into logical units?

☐ 13. Do you frequently lose points for not carefully checking your answers before turning them in?

☐ 14. Do you often lose points on true-false tests because you misread the questions?

☐ 15. Do you frequently daydream while studying for a test?

☐ 16. Do you depend primarily on last-minute cramming to prepare for tests?

Interpretation of the Survey

The preceding survey is not a foolproof measure of your study skills. However, it can give you an idea of problem areas. Or stated in athletic terms, it can give you an idea of what you need to correct in order to score better in academic competition. Count the checked boxes in each section. If you have five or more checks in a section, it is likely that you are weak in it. The rest of this book will help you to improve in these vital study skills areas.

HOW MUCH TIME?

No one will get more work done than you because he or she has more time than you. Everyone has the same amount of time each week—168 hours. What you do with your time will determine how successful you will be as a student and as an athlete. It is also important to remember that everyone plans and uses their time differently. The key to good planning is to create a schedule for yourself that takes into account your ability, your resources, and your needs. In other words, you should be selfish about your education.

Time is easy to waste and difficult to control. Most college freshmen experience a severe time shock. The time required to adequately do homework is double or triple what was needed in high school. A typical high achieving college freshman, for example, has to spend 4-6 study hours for a 3 hour course, and 2-3 laboratory hours for a 3 hour physical science course. Therefore, a freshman student with a 16 credit hour load (e.g. English, biology, mythology, sociology, physical education, and library skills) should set aside 28-33 hours a week for studying. This is equivalent to working on a part-time job. Indeed, your job is academic study. If you are also participating in a sport, your class, study, and practice-participation time commitments will exceed 60 hours a week (see Table 5-1).

TABLE 5-1

Sample Schedule

Courses				
Course	Hours	Time	Day	Location
ENG I	3	7:40- 8:30	M W F	203 AS
BIO I	5	12:40- 1:55	T R	Waters Aud.
BIO LAB	0	8:40- 9:30	R	322 Tucker
SOC I	3	10:40-11:30	M W F	102 PHYS
MYTH 60	3	9:40-10:30	M W F	319 GCP
LIB SKILLS	1	11:40-12:30	F	201 Ellis
PE (Ballet)	1	1:40- 2:30	M W	204 McKee
	16 Hours			

Study Time (Weekly)		
ENG I	6 Hours	• May vary week to week
BIO I	8 Hours	• Depends on individual needs
SOC I	6 Hours	Grade desired
MYTH	6 Hours	Subject background
LIB	1 Hour	
PE	1 Hour	• Vary with assignments
	28 Hours	

Sport Time		
M-F	Practice	15 Hours
Sat	Game	7 Hours
Sun	Films	2 Hours
		24 Hours

Sleep
8 Hours @ day—11:40-7:40 = 56 Hours @ week

Free Time
44 Hours @ week—How do you use it?

Source: Willis Ware and Chuck Patterson, *Missou Manual: Student Athlete's Handbook, 1983-84*, Columbia, MO: University of Missouri.

At first glance this may seem like an impossible situation, but it is not because these hours are spread over seven days. Even so, your schedule will be full—averaging 7-10 hours each day. With proper planning, however, you can have plenty of time to go to classes, do your homework, attend practice, get sufficient rest, and enjoy a wholesome social life. If you are like the majority of students, you have at least one of the following study problems.

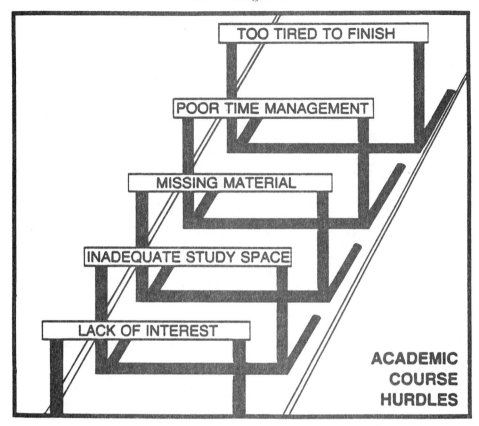

Figure 2. Academic course hurdles.

1. You do not get as much studying done as you should or your courses require. This is probably not because you do not try to study, but for whatever reason, you simply do not put in as much *quality time* as needed. In short, you waste time.
2. You attempt to study too many things and this results in wasted time. That is, you skip from one subject or activity to another without finishing any of them. You waste time.
3. You have great difficulty settling down to study. You seem to find an endless number of reasons to put off studying. Again, you waste time.

Each of these conditions can be corrected. First, you need a well-planned schedule that will allow you to use your time effectively. Remember, *time is the most valuable thing you have.* Once it is gone, you can never get it back. Try to not waste your time. A well-planned schedule can help you to make wise decisions, get started learning course material, tackle subjects you dislike, control your study breaks, increase your recreational and sport efficiency, and otherwise regulate your daily living.

NAME: Chuck Patterson

DATE: Aug. 24

COURSE	TEST	QUIZ	SPEECH	PAPER	STUDY TIME	TUTOR NEEDED
ENGLISH				WED	4	
BIO	THURS.				6	HELP!
BIO LAB					0	
SOC				MON	2	
MYTH	FRI				3	
LIB SK.					1	
P.E.					0	

	MON	TUES	WED	THURS	FRI	SAT	SUN
7:40	ENG.		ENG.		ENG.		
8:40				BIO LAB			
9:40	MYTH		MYTH		MYTH	PRE-GAME MEAL	
10:40	SOC		SOC.		SOC	↓	
11:40		LUNCH		LUNCH	LIB SK.		LUNCH
12:40	LUNCH	BIO LAB	LUNCH	BIO LAB	LUNCH	GAME	TRAINING
1:40	P.E.	BIO LAB	P.E.	BIO LAB			ROOM
2:40		1:55		1:55			↓
3:40	PRACTICE				→		FILMS
4:40						↓	
5:40	↓	↓	↓	↓	↓		
6:40	DINNER				↘		
7:40	STUDY HALL		BIO TUTOR	STUDY HALL			
8:40	|	ENG PAPER	↓	MYTH TEST			SOC PAPER
9:40	ENG PAPER	↓		STUDY!			
10:40							
11:40	SLEEP						

Figure 3. *Source*: Willis Ware and Chuck Patterson, *Missou Manual: Student Athlete's Handbook, 1983–84*, Columbia, MO: University of Missouri.

Your schedule can be an external motivator that pushes and pulls you into your subjects. If you have difficulty sitting down and studying, a schedule can help you to identify definite times for certain activities to begin and end. Our minds can and do play tricks on us. Without actually deciding to do so, we can push into the background doing work for difficult classes or classes we do not like. There is a tendency to spend most of our time on our favorite subjects.

A good schedule will minimize study time, recreation time, and sport time. If you are constantly doing one thing and thinking about another, you are likely to be doing both of them poorly. For example, if you are worried about a course while practicing your sport, your athletic performance will be negatively affected. You need to give adequate time to sports and courses. The first step is to determine the study activities you are currently engaged in and how much time is spent in these activities. To determine your present situation, answer the following questions:

- Am I spending enough time studying?
- Is any particular activity taking too much time?
- How much time do I spend on each course? How long does it take me to read an assignment in each course?
- Am I making consistent errors in estimating the amount of time needed for study?
- Do I use the time between classes efficiently?
- Do I have adequate planned breaks?
- Do I get too much or too little sleep?
- Do I get too much or too little recreation?
- How do I compare academically with my classmates?

After you have answered the questions listed above, you are ready to make a tentative weekly schedule. Usually a *minimum* time schedule is easier to follow. Plan only what needs to be done and later, if time permits and it is necessary, add other activities. In order to devise a good time schedule, you will have to know what courses you are taking, how much study time is needed for each course, and how much time is needed for sports, eating, and recreation. We recommend the following:

1. List all classes and other important activities such as eating, recreation, and sleep.
2. Schedule adequate study time (approximately two hours for each class hour). Use free periods between classes for studying.
3. Allow time for material preview and review.
4. Schedule study periods as close to each class as possible.
5. Do not schedule study periods for more than two hours, and take a 10-15 minute break each hour.

TABLE 5-2

Time Schedule

Based on the tips given to you in this chapter, make out a study schedule for yourself. It is wise to make at least one copy of your schedule—carry one with you and keep one in your room.

Hour	MON	TUES	WED	THURS	FRI	SAT	SUN
7:00							
8:00							
9:00							
10:00							
11:00							
12:00							
1:00							
2:00							
3:00							
4:00							
5:00							
6:00							
7:00							
8:00							
9:00							
10:00							
11:00							

6. If you borrow time from one scheduled activity to do another, replace it.
7. Be flexible. Alter your schedule as circumstances require. Plan your schedule so that it balances activities you dislike with those you like, easy courses with difficult courses, and work with play.
8. Keep your schedule where you can see it (see Table 5-2).

In the end, there is no magic formula for successful time management. You must have the determination and self-discipline to make your plan work. Don't expect miracles and don't give up after a brief trial period.

We cannot emphasize enough the importance of being realistic when making a schedule. This refers to both ends of the spectrum. At one end are students who schedule too little time for coursework, while at the other end are students who schedule too much time for their coursework. Some courses are easier for students to grasp than others. You have to determine the degree of difficulty each course has for you, not your classmates, and schedule your time accordingly.

Some students waste a lot of time trying to decide what to study and when to do it. The following account of Bill Dingobell illustrates this problem. He had a break from 9:20 a.m. until his sociology class began at 10:30 a.m.

9:20 Leaves class and walks to the library.
9:25 Arrives at the library and discovers that he left his sociology syllabus in his room.
9:35 Located a friend who had a copy of the sociology syllabus.
9:37 Starts looking for books needed to complete his homework.
9:40 Meets a student who is in his English class and talks to her about their English assignment.
9:42 Finishes conversation and continues search for sociology material.
9:47 Collects two of the three required books and starts back to his study table.
9:48 Stops in the snack room to get a candy bar; meets a coed he has been trying to date; buys her a soft drink.
10:00 Leaves the snack room and returns to study table.
10:02 Opens one of the books to an assigned page and then stares at the ceiling.
10:03 Closes book and picks up a copy of the student newspaper.
10:04 Puts paper down and starts a conversation with a teammate who is walking through the library.
10:11 Finishes conversation; decides to write the English assignment but discovers his pen is out of ink.
10:12 Lays head on table and closes his eyes.
10:15 Falls asleep.
10:27 Wakes up and rushes out of the library to sociology class.
10:36 Arrives late to class and sighs, "Not enough time to get all my work done."

Bill not only wasted his time but also his friends' time. He could have spent almost an hour reviewing his notes, reading his sociology assignment, or writing his English paper. Instead, he stumbled from one activity to another without doing any of his homework.

CONTROL YOUR STUDY ENVIRONMENT

Where you study is just as important as *how* and *when* you study. You must control your environment instead of letting it control you. If you do this, you will study in the best possible environment. Basically, this means finding a place where you can isolate or insulate yourself from distractions. Ideally, this place should be adequately furnished, properly ventilated, well lighted, and free of noise, visual distractions, and clutter. Few places are ideal, so you must learn to mentally shut out distractions. Of course, some students can study effectively with distractions. What kind of person are you?

Your study area should contain only the study material you need. It should also have a suitable chair and adequate working space. Sitting in a soft, plush chair may be comfortable but it can also be too comfortable—luring you to sleep. A comfortable straight-back chair is recommended. Whenever possible, avoid studying in bed or stretched out on a couch. As for study materials, make sure you have a dictionary, pencils or pens, paper, and erasers in your study area. And do not forget your books and other required reading or work materials.

Both natural and artificial lighting should be evenly distributed over your work surface, and the lighting should not be reflected in your eyes or cause a glare on the material you read. Indirect lighting is better than direct lighting. In order to prevent eyestrain, headache, and fatigue, avoid focusing lighting from lamps directly on the material you are reading.

The proper room temperature is neither too hot nor too cold. For most students, the ideal temperature for studying is between 70 and 75 degrees Fahrenheit. Rooms that are too hot or too cold can cause sleepiness, while those that are poorly ventilated can produce a feeling of mental fatigue. Your study area should be environmentally pleasing.

As a rule, it is better to have a special place that you use exclusively for study. If you use a place where you watch television or listen to records as your study place, you are likely to find it easy to stop studying and turn on the television or record player. That is why you should try to study in a room or space that you only associate with studying. In this regard, the library has a definite edge.

Set realistic goals for utilizing your time. You should know from past experience how long it takes you to work various kinds of problems, read various kinds of material, and write various kinds of reports. If you must err, *overestimate* rather than underestimate, the time you require for specific projects. Like improving athletic performances, it is better to increase your academic goals in small manageable units. And be prepared for set-backs in your progress. There will be days when you will not be able to achieve even your original goals. The "secret" is not to give up.

Devise a way to "psych" yourself into studying. Just as some athletes wear a particular pair of socks or shirt or jewelry during practice, you may have to do the same thing during study periods. It could be a particular piece of clothing. Or it could be a particular object placed on your work area to designate to you and others that you are about the business of studying. Use your study symbol only for studying. There will be times when you will have to politely tell your friends not to bother you.

Don't begin your study sessions by complaining about your lack of interest in studying or your inability to understand the assignment. When you become an "I can't" student, you have lost the edge. If you start day-dreaming once you begin studying, stand up and walk around for a brief while. This will help to refocus your attention to your assignment. Decide the order in which your study will be done and begin.

If you do not already do it, develop the habit of setting aside a certain time each day to study. This time is likely to vary according to your class schedule, but it should be consistent and rigorously followed. This is exactly what you do for your athletic activities. And like athletics, follow your schedule even when you do not want to. Most athletes would rather play their sport in competition than practice it. Yet it is practice that allows you to master your sport and improve your game performance. Academics are no different. Studying can help you to excel in your courses or, at least, to improve your performance.

Finish all current assignments before moving on to new ones. Do an assignment until you get it right. If you need help, ask for it. Relatedly, most students spend too much of their time worrying about unfinished non-academic business when they should be studying. Finish what you have begun before you start studying, and try to not start nonacademic projects or personal conversations that are likely to require a large time commitment just before it is time to begin studying.

Divide your study goals into several short-range projections. These projections should ultimately lead to the completion of a final project. This will divide the task into manageable pieces. For example, if a term paper is due at the end of the semester, divide your study sessions into projected research and completed pages. Students frequently become immobilized by the thought of completing an assignment, while they are not frightened by bits and pieces of it. You do not get dressed all at once. You put on one piece at a time. Like getting dressed, your assignments can be completed in small units—one piece at a time. Thus, a 400 page book can be read 40 pages each study time.

Keep a reminder sheet or reminder pad handy so that you can remember things that need to be done. This pad is also the place you can jot down things you discover and want to use or look up at a later date. Do not trust your memory—write things down. In summary:

- Locate and use a special place to study.
- Set specific goals (start and finish) for completing assignments.
- Select a study symbol (clothing or other object) and make it part of your study ritual.
- Begin each study session with a positive attitude.
- If you start daydreaming, stop studying and walk around for a brief time.

- Set aside certain times for studying.
- Try to finish all nonacademic business started just before you begin studying.
- Establish short-range study subgoals.
- Keep a reminder pad handy.

Techniques and Tips

There are many other helpful ideas and techniques for successful time management. Listed below is a summary of some of them. Not all of the items on the checklist may pertain to you. As you read through them, put a checkmark in the box beside each item in which you need to improve. Then try to practice the suggested time management techniques.

☐ 1. **Decide to get organized.** Have you said to yourself that you have got to get organized but nothing happened? In all probability nothing happened because you didn't make a conscious decision that getting organized is really important. Like learning a sport or a new play or a new position, you have got to convince yourself that time management in academics is essential to your success. First, you must believe in academic time management.

☐ 2. **Analyze your time habits.** Find out how you really spend your time. This can be done by keeping track of everything you do in a selected week. Jot down your exact academic activities in time units, e.g. every 15 minutes, 30 minutes, or hour write down what you have done. At the end of the week, analyze how you spent your time. Ask yourself how much each of the activities contributed to academic goals you considered important. Rate the activities on a scale ranging from 1 to 10, with 10 being the most helpful activities and 1 being the least helpful. This can allow you to get in touch with your good and bad study habits.

☐ 3. **Devise a schedule.** Near the end of each day, write down the things you plan to do the next day. List high priority things at the top of your list and low priority things at the bottom. Do not include the time-wasters you uncovered when you analyzed your time habits. Cross off each item as you complete it. Try to finish your top priority items before moving to low priority items. The key is to set priorities for your time and energy.

☐ 4. **Set deadlines.** If you believe in the importance of the various tasks you set out to complete, this will motivate you to do them. Set realistic deadlines for yourself but stay flexible. If your schedule calls for accomplishing a difficult task and you don't have the energy or resources to do it, move to another priority item. A change in your schedule may energize you. When your energy is low, it is better to do routine rather than difficult tasks. You can do certain things better at certain times. Learn to recognize when your moods, feelings, and academic energy levels are high or low, but do not allow this to be an excuse for doing nothing. Sometimes you have to study in pain.

☐ 5. **Make a time goal plan.** It is not very helpful for you to decide to "get a lot of work done" unless you decide on getting *specific* work done. Try to finish each task within the projected period. Do not abandon your plan merely because the material is difficult. This is a sign of a poor academic game plan.

☐ 6. **Do not overplan.** One of the common mistakes students make is to assume that they can do more in a given time period than they actually can. When this happens, you are likely to panic and rush through things without doing anything adequately. It is important that you are realistic about your abilities and what you can do within a given amount of time.

☐ 7. **Know your best work time.** Some people are "early birds," others are "afternoon cats," and others are "night owls." When are you in top academic form? Try to devise your study schedule during your most efficient time. For example, if you are a morning person, try to get up early enough to do most of your studying.

☐ 8. **Cancel your schedule sometimes.** Sometimes you may have to put forth a superhuman effort to complete an assignment. This requires long hours and little relaxation. Do not make this a habit but realize that cram sessions are used for academic survival by even the best students. Provide balance in your schedule. If you alter or cancel it to cram in work, do the same thing for relaxation and recreation. A good rule of thumb is to always find something fun to do during your school year.

☐ 9. **Use waiting time.** Waiting is an aspect of life. We are always waiting for someone or something. If you plan ahead, you can use this time to read assignments, write and revise reports, and revise your schedule. Do not use waiting as an excuse to avoid class assignments. The longer you wait to start or finish projects, the less likely it is that you will finish them. By forcing yourself to use waiting time constructively, you allow studying to become a habit. Do not wait for an external inspiration to use waiting time. Be your own inspiration.

☐ 10. **Do not live in the past.** Past mistakes are valuable lessons to be learned from, but you cannot change the past. You may be able to do better today and tomorrow. You will never know if you do not try. Too much mental replaying of academic failures can lead to a negative attitude about school. Focus on your strengths. Do not be afraid to make mistakes—learn from them.

THE ACADEMIC GAME PLAN

There are three basic tools of a college education: (1) time, (2) teachers, and (3) books. You must learn to use these tools correctly.

Good students are not "born students"; they are made by continuous and diligent study. There is no short cut to academic success. First, *you must want to be a good student.* Second, *you must use your time and resources properly.* This means knowing what you are going to do and when you are going to do it. In short, you must have an academic game plan—a carefully worked out study schedule and academically sound procedures for writing papers and taking tests. These are prerequisites to earning good grades. Most students wonder where their time goes, but few of them analyze their behavior in order to find out. Only by honestly evaluating your use of time will you be able to devise an effective academic game plan.

As in sports, it is essential that you have a plan of action. Students who develop systematic and regular study habits and budget their time properly increase their ability to get good grades. A schedule that is followed soon becomes an easy routine, and constant repetition becomes a habit. Of course, constant repetition of wasting time is a bad habit. Too many students have bad study habits. Like body building, a carefully designed study schedule is mind building.

You should base your academic game plan on realistic factors: What are your interests? What are your capabilities? What are your athletic commitments? Only you can create a plan that is optimally effective for you. When you are practicing your sport or preparing for a class, you are working for yourself. Often, students complain that they have to write a report or read a chapter for a teacher. Wrong! Students do homework for themselves. You do a lot of work in school, but none of it is for a teacher. You are working to develop *yourself.*

Your instructors are also working for you. They know the course material; you do not. Their job is to share their knowledge with you. Listen carefully to what they say, note the things they consider important, and pay attention when they explain the "difficult parts." You must learn to distinguish between essential and nonessential course materials. Always remember that what an instructor does in a class has a primary purpose—to help you learn. If you must designate a foe in this process, designate yourself. You may be your own worst enemy.

The textbook is probably the greatest single source of information available to students. Almost all classroom activities center on textbook material. Books are the common ground on which students and instructors meet. You will spend more hours studying books than any other form of material. While the subjects, nature, and complexity of books vary greatly, the fundamental techniques for successful study are basically the same for all books.

The textbook is the foundation upon which you must build your education. If you do not read your textbooks, then your education will not be complete. Most textbooks are arranged as a guide to take you from one important point to another. Thus, each book is a series of mental stepping stones leading to knowledge. The index, definitions, charts and tables, rules, and footnotes or endnotes all are part of the learning process. When you ignore them, you guarantee yourself not to fully comprehend the book's content. The following suggestions may help you better use your textbooks.

- Unless school property, own your books and write your name and address in them.
- Know the names of the authors of your books and, if possible, something about them.
- Briefly skim each book, paying particular attention to contents, chapter titles, section headings, tables, and illustrations.
- Think of your textbook as cumulative knowledge to be learned and not as so many pages to be read or avoided.

Now you are ready to implement an academic game plan. The chapters that follow will provide you with more specifics. As a prelude, check the box in front of each activity that you are currently doing.

☐ 1. *Go to class.* Unless you are sick or traveling with your team or have some other official excuse, attend your classes.

☐ 2. *Get a notebook or folder for each course.*

☐ 3. *Get a calendar and write in all important information* such as
- Due dates for assignments.
- Dates of quizzes and examinations.
- Appointments with advisors, instructors, coaches, and other persons.
- Team travel dates.
- Vacations.

☐ 4. *Get required textbooks for each course and read them.*

☐ 5. *Keep all course handouts and notes and periodically review them.*

☐ 6. *Try to make thorough class notes, but do not let this distract you from listening to all of the lecture.*

☐ 7. *Do not wait until the day before a test or an assignment is due to study or, if needed, to ask for a tutor.*

☐ 8. *Do not ask tutors to do your assignments for you. Nor should you expect a tutor to adequately help you in one cram session.*

☐ 9. *Organize your time so that you do not have to complete several major projects on the same day.* Plan ahead and budget your time.

☐ 10. *Get to know your instructors.* Visit them immediately after class or during their office hours if you are:

- Confused about course material.
- Doing poorly and need guidance to improve.
- Dissatisfied with some aspect of the course.
- Pleased with the course.

☐ 11. *If possible, get together at least once a week with a student in your class or a tutor to review your course material. During these sessions, do not copy someone else's work and turn it in as your own.*

☐ 12. *Do not be afraid to ask for help or to admit failure.* A problem cannot be solved if it is not acknowledged.

☐ 13. *Study, study, study.*

Make a schedule and stick to it until you revise it.

Chapter 6

LISTENING AND MAKING NOTES

Most students are not exposed to extensive lecturing prior to entering college. Therefore, very few freshmen know how to make good lecture notes. Contrary to popular opinion, few instructors simply repeat what is in the assigned textbooks. Rather, they expand on the information by adding more details and providing different and sometimes unique interpretations. Lecture notes can aid you in understanding instructors' presentations and also aid in preparing for course examinations. If you elect to sleep or tune out an instructor, you are likely to be ensuring yourself a low grade.

The average student spends about 5 percent of his or her course time talking; 10 percent writing; 30 percent reading; and 55 percent listening. These statistics are ample reasons you would be wise to develop your listening skills.

What instructors say and *how* they say it can tell you a lot about a course and the instructors, too. When you give an instructor your full and undivided attention, you have taken the first step in effective (good) listening. A general rule is: Look at your instructor and not the chalk board, other students, the floor, or ceiling unless directed to do so by your instructor. There are many ways you can develop good listening skills. We will discuss a few of them in the following sections.

AVOIDING LISTENING DISTRACTIONS

With practice and determination, you can master the art of listening. In order to do this, you must focus your mental energies on listening and gear your listening to produce an *active response*. This means learning to sustain your attention while listening by eliminating mental filters and barriers that prevent you from receiving the complete message. First, if you have it, rid yourself of the false belief that listening is only a matter of hearing. Listening is more than hearing—it is *giving sounds the same meanings that they have for the sender of the message.* Listening does not occur in the ears; it takes place between the ears. In short, listening is a mental process.

Communication occurs only when the person sending a message and the individual receiving it have the same picture in their minds. This is the objective of all communication. It is not uncommon for an instructor to misinterpret student silence as communication. Often what has happened is that the students are too embarrassed to admit they did not understand a portion or all of the lecture.

If a good speaker speaks with his or her whole body, then it is also true that a good listener listens with his or her whole body. Body posture, facial expressions, open and closed hands, and position of the head can all contribute to effective listening. If you do not feel comfortable verbally telling an instructor that you are having problems with the lecture, you can do it in a polite nonverbal way, e.g. a frown or searching eyes. Fear of the instructor is a barrier to learning.

Perhaps the most important act in listening is to avoid or resist distractions. If there is a distraction to your listening, recognize it and deal with it. Just as you have to resist people and situations that encourage you to miss practice, you must also not yield to temptation to miss classes. Unless you have an official excuse, you should always go to class. While in class, it is wise to avoid anything that will take your attention away from the instructor. In short, position yourself in such a way as to avoid distracting people, noises, and views. Dealing quickly with distractions is the best way to sustain your attention. Above all else, you should make a conscious effort to pay attention to your instructors. It is easier to pay attention when there is a pay-off.

In order to maximize your education, you must know why you are enrolled in a particular course. That is, you should have a selfish reason for listening to your instructors and learning the material. The reason, of course, is to become better educated. If you are going to learn the course material, you must be able to pick out the *who, what, where, when, why,* and *how* facts in lectures. To do this, you have to focus not only on an instructor's words but also relate them to assigned readings.

Every course you enroll in should lead to fulfilling your degree requirements. Make sure that you are enrolled in courses that will count toward a degree and not just courses that will keep you eligible. If you are uncertain about the relevance of a course, ask the chairperson of the department in which you desire to get a degree. The greatest distraction to listening is being in a course that leads nowhere. Find out how your participation in every academic course can lead to the ultimate victory— graduation.

Listen to your instructors so that you can respond appropriately during discussions and examinations. When an instructor begins lecturing, it is important that you initially suspend your own personal judgment. This means that you should try to accept the instructor's physical appearance, tone of voice, manner of delivery, and selection of material. If you are going to listen to what a speaker has to say, you must let his or her message reach you in as clear a form as possible. Initially, trust the instructor to be conscientious and knowledgeable enough to present what you need to know in order to master the course. Later, your opinion of the instructor may change, but until you have heard what he or she has to say and you have enough familiarity with the course content to evaluate it, be a learner, not a critic. Write down your questions and points of disagreement for future reference and discussion.

It is normal to judge or evaluate everything we hear. When someone lectures, before they have barely begun expressing their ideas, we tend to decide whether or not they are correct. We become so busy engaging in our own mental process of evaluation that we no longer hear what is being said. When this happens, we stop listening and start our own mental rebuttal of the speaker. We stop learning!

Another disruptive listening habit is the tendency to jump to conclusions—to fill in the details before the speaker finishes talking. This is putting words into other peoples' mouths, and it is related to the fact that we all are so firmly entrenched in certain beliefs and values that we attribute them to other people. We do not just put any words into other peoples' mouths; we put *our words* into their mouths. Probably one of the most common and most serious blocks to effective listening is the closed mind. We simply do not want to listen to anything contrary to our own beliefs. This is not to say that you should believe everything you hear. However, you should acquire all the pertinent information *before* making any conclusions. The proper order of reasoning is to (1) understand, (2) evaluate, and then (3) judge. Below are the Ten Commandments of Effective Listening:

1. You should neither judge nor evaluate other persons until you understand them.
2. You should not attribute your own thoughts or ideas to the speaker.
3. You should not infer thoughts, facts, or ideas in addition to those stated by the speaker.
4. You should not permit your thoughts to stray nor your mind to wander during a lecture.
5. You should not close your mind to the speaker.
6. You should not permit your prejudices and biases to block your reasoning.
7. You should not interpret the speaker's words and phrases except as they are interpreted by him or her.

8. You should not talk when the speaker is talking.
9. You should not consider yourself too good to learn from any person.
10. You should not fear improvement, correction, or change.

Nor should you forget that in most courses the instructors are not concerned with what you believe or whether you agree with them. Your grade will be based on your ability to demonstrate an understanding of class lectures and course assignments. Each year, many students fail courses because they refuse to accept an instructor's appearance. You should guard against personalizing your reactions to how an instructor looks. Approach your biases in the following manner.

General Appearance

Make a conscious effort to discount the lecturer's size, weight, complexion, dress, and posture. When you are confronted with what to you is a physically unattractive instructor, say to yourself, "This man (woman) may have something important to say. I am going to try to find out what it is."

Attitude

Remind yourself that if your instructor is flippant, overbearing, argumentative, or arrogant, these characteristics are habitual and difficult to correct. Usually, such behavior is not intentional. Say to yourself, "This instructor's attitude does not affect what he (she) has to say. It only colors how it is said. I shall do everything I can to dig beneath his (her) attitude—to separate his (her) ideas from the outward impression I have gotten."

Voice and Mannerisms

A voice that gets on your nerves or a nervous twitch, for example, can detract from the lecture. These things do not affect the real value of what your instructor has to offer. Say to yourself, "These habits have no relationship to what he (she) is saying. I will try to not let myself be influenced by these superficial things."

Language and Speech Characteristics

Instructors who speak with an accent or a dialect are sometimes ridiculed by students. Admittedly, they may be difficult to understand during their presentations, but this is not a valid reason for you to routinely tune them out. Say to yourself, "This will not be easy, but I am going to try extra hard to understand the lectures. If I do not understand, I will ask for clarification of specific sentences."

Sex and Ethnicity

Some students have hang-ups about being taught by female instructors; other students prefer not to be taught by ethnic minority instructors. There is no place in education for bigotry. Say to yourself, "I am here to get an education and, I will accept my instructor's gender (ethnicity) without trying to demean her (him)."

Other Distractions

Don't depend on someone else's opinion of an instructor's competence or quality of presentations. An individual may have been a poor lecturer last semester, realized it, and improved. If you tune him out, how will you know that he has not greatly improved? In the same vein, he may have been great last semester but a poor lecturer this semester. Do not be distracted by reputations or style. Hear each instructor out. Athletes do not always perform at the same level, neither do teachers.

By now it should be clear that listening is hard work, and it requires considerable concentration. Student athletes, more so than most nonathletes, understand hard work and intense concentration. As an athlete, you have learned how to (1) listen to your coaches and teammates, (2) blot out distractions, and (3) read subtle nonverbal cues of your critics. Now, you must do it in academic settings.

It may be difficult for you to listen to most instructors because they speak at rates between 100 and 150 words per minute but you listen at a rate three or four times faster. That is why in most lecture situations your mind may start to wander to other things. It is normal to get tired waiting for an instructor's next important thoughts. Instead of abandoning an instructor once you grasp what he or she has said, try to use your extra listening time to mentally (1) anticipate what he or she will say next, (2) summarize what has been said, and (3) reflect on and weigh the importance of what has been said.

Listening is difficult because most of us have learned not to hear or listen to other persons. We are conditioned to hear only what we want to hear. Thus, we are easily distracted in courses because we want to be. And we sometimes distort instructors' messages because we want to. Some student-athletes are afraid that if they really listen to their teachers, they will enjoy the courses. Heaven forbid they should learn something! This attitude and behavior supports the *dumb jock stereotype*. Athletes are no different from their classmates in ability. Unfortunately, some athletes give up too soon on themselves as students. When they give up, they behave like the negative stereotype.

There are valid reasons you may be hesitant to get actively involved in classroom lectures and campus activities. Through your involvement, you incur the following risks:

- The risk of being "put down" or ridiculed.
- The risk of being outreasoned.
- The risk of changing your opinions and behavior.
- The risk of failing.
- The risk of exposing your real self.

These risks are great but the rewards are greater for individuals who take them and learn their subjects. In order to do this, you must understand your instructors' lectures.

UNDERSTAND WHAT YOU HEAR

If you have difficulty understanding course lectures, you usually are not alone. But even if you were the only one who did not understand the lectures, do not be ashamed of that fact. Be ashamed, however, if you do not ask the instructor or a tutor for help. It is better to ask what to you may *seem* to be "dumb" or "stupid" questions than to get grades that indicate that you *are* dumb or stupid. Listed below are five recommendations for behavior that will help you to understand what you hear.

1. *Rephrase your understanding of what the instructor was trying to say in your own words and, whenever necessary, check with the instructor.* Most instructors expect to be misunderstood by a few students, and they welcome questions for clarification. Put aside your false pride or, more likely, fear of instructors and ask your questions. The best way to minimize misunderstanding is to tell the instructor in your own words what you heard him or her say.

2. *When you disagree with an instructor or dislike the assignment or materials presented, make an extra effort to understand what has been said.* Often, we are so committed to our own ideas and values that we reject new ideas, values, and behavior without understanding them. You do not have to agree with a point of view but if it is part of your course material, you need to understand it. Openly disagreeing with an instructor in order to win an argument may make you feel good, but this can often detract your attention from the instructor's lectures. Periodically consider whether you are giving the words or phrases of instructors whom you do not like meanings different from what were intended. Also consider whether your instructors have more or better information than you. They usually do! You should listen harder when you disagree with your instructors.

3. *If you find something in a lecture exciting, watch out for error of exaggeration in your understanding of it.* When most people get excited, they want to stay that way. Do not leap to the conclusion that because you like what an instructor says in one lecture, you will like everything else he or she says. Listen carefully to what is said in all lectures. Besides, you may be incorrectly interpreting the lectures.

4. *If you find a lecture boring, watch out for errors of transposition.* "Transposition" means reversing the order of things. When you disarrange a message, you distort it, and you will have difficulty understanding it. If you become aware that your attention has wandered and you may have misinterpreted the instructor, seek him or her out for clarification. In addition to causing a disordering of these items in a lecture, boredom can also cause an emphasis shift from one place in a lecture to another. This can change the entire meaning of the message. When in doubt, check it out.

5. *Concentrate on unfamiliar items in a lecture.* Most students feel bored when they believe they are being told something they already know. You should listen to the lecture to find *unfamiliar* information. Sometimes this is like looking for a needle in a haystack. The unfamiliar can usually be found hidden under overfamiliar material. Students who tune in the lecture and do not tune out the lecturer are least likely to miss these important points. You should listen with special care whenever someone seems to be telling you something you already know. This is a good academic practice, and after you leave college it will be a profitable business practice.

GUIDE TO EFFECTIVE LISTENING

An old saying goes something like this: "I know you think you understand what I said, but what you said is not what I meant." Too many students get low grades because of misunderstood lectures. The following guide to effective listening can help you to understand instructors:

1. *Become interested in the subject.* Your listening effectiveness is increased when you are interested in what is being discussed. As you listen to a class lecture, be alert for information that may be useful to you. Bits and pieces of information can add up to total comprehension of a course.

2. *Become an active listener.* Effective lecturers have an organization to what they say. There is usually a beginning, a middle, and an end to each of their lectures. Sandwiched between these parts are the data relevant to passing the course. The essential aspects of a lecture are found not only in verbal communication but also in the instructor's nonverbal messages. Nonverbal communication includes gestures, tone and volume of voice, eye contact, and body positions. You must learn to "hear" with your eyes as well as with your ears when attending a lecture.

3. *Listen for ideas.* Good listeners focus on important ideas; they do not try to memorize all of a lecture.

4. *Be prepared.* Read the assignment and previous notes you have taken before coming to the lecture. You do this in sports, so why not do it in your courses, too?

5. *Be flexible.* When recording what you hear, shift your method of making notes to fit the instructor's method of delivery. Some lectures can be outlined, some can be captured with a few key words or phrases, and others can be copied almost word-for-word.

A good listener does not call a course "uninteresting." There is interesting, usable information in all courses. Your challenge is to find it. Some instructors are experts in hiding the interesting parts of their lectures. Few instructors will tell you to "write this down" or "this is a major point," but most of them will give clear signals regarding various aspects of their course lectures. Examples of common signals include:

"There are four aspects of this..." (get ready)
"First...Second...Third...Fourth..." (there they are)
"And the most significant..." (in case you do not know)

Some instructors signal when supportive material is forthcoming:

"For example..."
"Similarly..."
"For instance..."
"Furthermore..."

Some instructors signal conclusions and summaries:

"In conclusion..."
"Finally..."
"Therefore..."
"As a result..."
"It is evident..."

Some instructors signal very loudly:

"The major point is..."
"Remember that..."
"It is important to remember..."
"Contrary to popular opinion..."
"You'll see this later..."

Often these signals are missed or ignored by students who have not learned to listen effectively. As noted earlier, good listening is an active process. There is no such thing as an effective passive listener. Like reading, effective listening involves active concentration and continuous evaluation. This is the process of continuously connecting what an instructor says with what you have learned before and believe.

EFFECTIVE NOTE-MAKING SKILLS

Check the boxes in front of the statements that apply to you.
☐ 1. I seldom take notes in class.
☐ 2. I usually write so much that I miss a lot of what my instructors say.
☐ 3. I do not take a notebook to all of my classes.
☐ 4. My attention often wanders during classes.
☐ 5. I often have difficulty deciphering my lecture notes.
☐ 6. Sometimes I do not take enough notes.
☐ 7. I have never been able to organize my notes.

☐ 8. I do a lot of doodling during class.
☐ 9. It is difficult for me to follow the organization of a lecture.
☐ 10. I seldom have the important points in my notes.
☐ 11. I usually use a pencil for making class notes.
☐ 12. I sometimes lose papers from my lecture notes.

There are ample research studies and college professors to attest to the importance of making good class notes. Most students who make president's and dean's lists have learned to include almost everything which will be asked in quizzes. When done well, notemaking has the following functions: (1) It is a device for controlling student attention so that ideas are recorded in proportion to their value and (2) it is an aid to memory. When you make good notes on a lecture, book, or class discussion, your retention is improved. Recording what is said and going on in a class is bound to impress you with the significance of the events, as well as to provide you with material for later reviews.

Notes are of relatively little value when the instructor is reading or reciting very simple and interesting concepts. You will easily remember these things. Unfortunately, few lectures are very simple and even fewer are interesting to all students. The subject matter is usually abstract, condensed, and impersonal and, therefore, difficult to attend to continuously. Each class lecture tends to be related to previous lectures. Thus, notes can give you a complete record of the total course.

Some authors compare notes to the log of a ship: They are records of intellectual voyages, containing references to important events and points covered. It is impossible without written records for students to remember lecture material. (Most classes on the semester system meet approximately 150 minutes a week.) Both the *form* and the *content* of lecture notes are crucial to learning, although, in most instances, the content is more essential. In order to make the content as meaningful as possible, you must learn to listen critically and to evaluate the information being given, rather than to try to write down every word. It is also important that you write the notes in your own words, unless you must memorize the exact words, e.g. definitions, formulas and poetry.

Good notes require *selection* and *organization*. First, you must select the statements that are most essential to your understanding the material. Second, you must organize these statements into a system of ideas that will make sense to you at a later date. This is the process of *making good notes* as opposed to *taking good notes*. The following activities will improve your note-making skills.

1. **Prepare to listen**
   • Read previous lecture notes before going to class.
   • Read the assignment for which the lecture is to be given.
   • Formulate questions you want answered.

- Take all the materials you need to class, e.g. notebook, pencils and pen, and textbooks.
- Use a pen to make your notes.
- Arrive early, sit where you can see the instructor and the chalkboard, and where you can be seen and heard.

2. **Listening-writing**
   - Listen critically to all that is said and sort out main ideas.
   - Know the instructor's values.
   - Separate your thoughts and opinions from the instructor's.
   - Write neatly and abbreviate freely.
   - Copy everything that your instructor writes on the board.
   - Ask for clarification if you do not understand material.

3. **Review**
   - Immediately after class, review your notes and fill in missing data.
   - If necessary, reorganize and rewrite your notes.

You should try several forms of notes so that you can select the appropriate ones for each course. Instructors use different types of organization for their lectures. One may talk "off the top of his/her head," while another may follow a well-constructed outline, and a third may speak from a written manuscript. Try to determine the kind of organization each of your instructors uses so that you can be better prepared for his or her lectures.

This problem is compounded because instructors have varying types of lecture delivery. Some speak quickly and others speak slowly; some focus on specifics, while others talk in generalities; some follow the course syllabus, while others do not; some follow the textbook topic for topic, while others seldom refer to the textbook. This does not mean that one method of presenting course material is better than another. If simply means that instructors utilize diverse ways to present their course content. Once you discover your instructor's organization and style of delivery, you can decide how to organize your own notes. Generally, notes should be as legible, brief, and comprehensive as possible. Do not make the mistake of writing down only the things you do not understand. Your notes should be written within the context of material presented—familiar and unfamiliar.

There are many many kinds of notes. Some are more helpful than the others. The key to making notes is for you to make the best notes for each course. With this thought in mind, we offer the following types of notes as an illustration.

1. A complete duplication of the lecture.
2. A summary of ideas with some words and sentences omitted.
3. Diagrams, tables, and drawings with occasional comments.
4. A list of topics discussed, without reference to details.

5. Questions and answers.
6. The outline form—a logical organization of topics and subtopics.

Technically, a complete duplication of a lecture is not a note; it is a copy. Unless the instructor speaks very slowly and you have excellent stenographic skills, you will not be able to make duplications of lectures. There are, however, times when portions of lectures should be copied verbatim. Examples of such material are quoted passages, rules, recipes, and theorems. In most instances, instructors will slow up their presentation so that you can copy the exact wording. In all other cases, where exact wording is not required, you should use some form of abbreviation or rewording. Paraphrasing requires more active listening than complete duplication (see Figures 4 and 5).

Summaries of ideas are very common types of notes. If they are carefully done (all of the facts included), summary notes are excellent references. It requires constant thought and critical judgment to produce good abbreviated notes. A foremost advantage of good abbreviated notes is that they are concise and coherent. A major disadvantage is that these notes impede a quick review of the course because the missing data have to be filled in.

Occasional comments, diagrams or tables are used by many students. Unless you have good recall, this form of notes will be difficult for you to put into the perspective of the total lectures. Students in science classes tend to list topics with brief notes on each. Question and answer notes are a good method for recording class discussions. The outline method requires clear, logical thinking. The essence of outlining is that the student learns to pick out major and minor points. Most students use a mixture of note forms.

EDITING LECTURE NOTES

Shortly after the notes have been made, you should spend 5 to 10 minutes reviewing and editing them. This is the best time to make additions and changes because the material is fresh in your memory. The longer you wait, the more you will forget and distort what you heard. In summary, there are two good reasons for reviewing your notes as soon as possible after the lecture:

1. Unless you review your notes within 24 hours after the lecture or at the latest before the next lecture, your retention will drop considerably. After this time, you will be relearning instead of reviewing.
2. By recalling what parts of the lecture were unclear, you can ask the instructor or your classmates for clarification or you can consult your textbook or additional readings for further information.

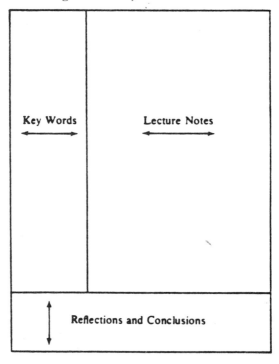

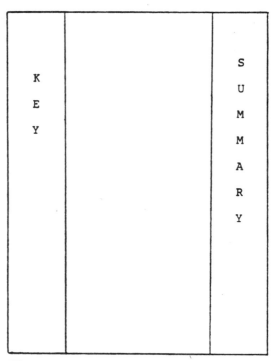

Figure 4. Sample margins for lecture notes.

March 29   P.3

SOCIAL GROUPS

A <u>social group</u> exists when members = united
by <u>emotional</u> <u>solidarity</u> and <u>common</u> <u>purpose</u>

Emotional | <u>Small group</u> = 2-30 persons, usually 2-15.
Solidarity |
Effective | I. Characteristics of <u>effective</u> <u>group</u>:
          | 1. Knows why it exists
          | 2. Creates good work atmosphere
          | 3. Has decision-making guidelines
          | 4. Allows everyone to contribute
          | 5. Has effective communication
          | 6. Members give and receive help
          | 7. Can cope with <u>conflict</u>
          | _____
          | <u>Note</u>: 1. Group membership = primary source
          | of security for individual. (EX.)
Attitudes | Determines self-esteem and social
Beliefs | status. 2. Every group requires
Values | conformity in <u>attitudes</u>, <u>beliefs</u>
          | and <u>values</u>.

*** Must be able to give examples of several types of small
groups based on characteristics listed above.

Figure 5. Marked lecture note.

When going over your notes, underline key statements and important concepts. You can also use asterisks, stars, and other signal marks to indicate important concepts. Use your margins to highlight information (see Figure 5). One of the margins can be a *key* to important names, dates, concepts, formulas, and so forth. This will provide you with specific facts that you can use to develop reports. The other margin can be used to write a brief *summary* of the topics on the page. This will help you to relate the contents on the page to the current lecture or to other lectures, and it will prepare you for quizzes and examinations.

Grading Your Notes

The final test of notes is your ability to use them to pass examinations and write papers. However, occasionally good note makers do poorly in examinations. In most instances, this is because they spend an inadequate amount of time reviewing their notes and reciting them.

Evaluation of Notes

There are four basic characteristics of good notes: complete, logical and coordinated parts, accurate, and attractive in form. Ask a friend to grade your notes by checking all of the boxes below that best describe them.

1. **Complete**
   - ☐ In general, they are complete.
   - ☐ Too wordy or repetitious.
   - ☐ Lacking in many essential details.
   - ☐ Inadequate in use of diagrams, illustrations, etc.

2. **Logical and Coordinated Parts**
   - ☐ The organization is satisfactory.
   - ☐ Illogical selection of topics.
   - ☐ Subtopics poorly worded.

3. **Accurate**
   - ☐ Basically the notes are accurate.
   - ☐ Has a few inaccuracies.
   - ☐ Has numerous inaccuracies.
   - ☐ Contains prejudices which cause misinterpretations.

4. **Attractive Form**
   - ☐ The form is satisfactory.
   - ☐ Illegible in places.
   - ☐ Not neat—has blots and smears.
   - ☐ Cramped or congested writing.

Notebooks

There are many good notebooks and you should select the one that you feel most comfortable using. A notebook that a friend owns may not be what you should own. Good notebooks, like good shoes, should fit you. Try them before settling on one. There are some fairly standard recommendations for using notebooks:

1. *Use a standard (8½" x 11") looseleaf or spiral-type notebook.* Reasons for this recommendation include:
   - Larger notebooks are too bulky for carrying and difficult to write on if a room has chairs with narrow arm rests.
   - Smaller notebooks require too many pages and tend to result in cramped writing.
   - Papers you turn in to your instructor should be the same size as typed term papers.
2. *Do not use loose sheets of paper, yellow pads, or writing tablets.* These items are too easily lost or damaged.
3. *Place your name, address, and telephone number in each notebook.* This will allow individuals to return your property if you lose it and they find it.
4. *Number each page.* This will assist you in retrieving information.
5. *Keep each course separated from the others.* Do this either by separate notebooks, dividers, or tabs.
6. *Use one side of the page only.* The other side can be used for note revisions, comments, questions, and notes to yourself.
7. *Always use an ink pen.* Ink is less likely to smudge and is easier to read than pencil.
8. *Enter the date on each class lecture page.* This will help you to locate material.

Since notes are made best in notebooks, your academic equipment should include notebooks. A cluttered, dirty, poorly organized notebook will not be much help to you. If you are not going to properly use notebooks, we suggest that you invest your money and energy in something else.

Notebook Evaluation

Evaluate your notebooks in terms of the characteristics listed below. Check the box in front of each characteristic that describes your notebooks.

☐ Spiral-type or looseleaf notebooks are used.
☐ Notes are written in ink.
☐ Notes are free of doodling.
☐ Notes are legible.
☐ Notes are written on one side.

☐ Each course is separated.
☐ Lecture and reading notes are separated.
☐ All notes have your name written at the top of them.
☐ Pages are numbered.
☐ Lectures notes are dated.
☐ Adequate abbreviation throughout the notes.
☐ Notes are evenly spaced.
☐ Does not have too many notes.
☐ Important points are set off (underlined, highlighted, numbered, asterisks, stars, exclamation point, etc.) but not excessively.

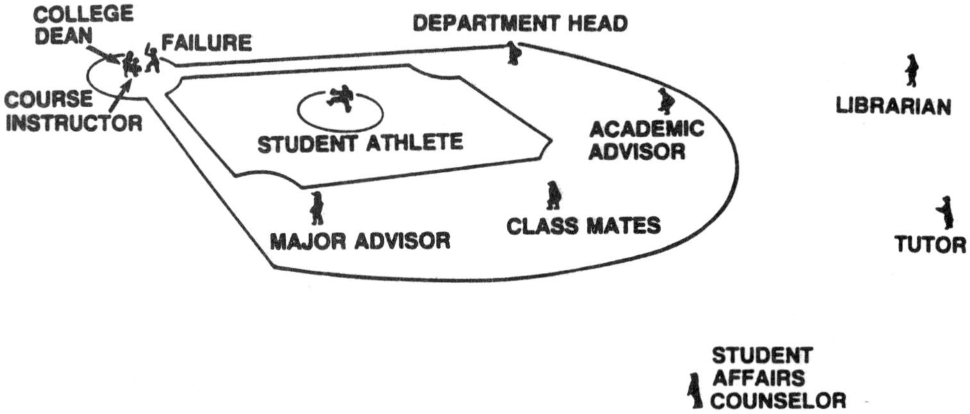

Figure 6. Line up to prevent academic failure.

PREPARING FOR TESTS

T here are several reasons for tests and examinations, and the least of these is for your instructor to have an excuse to give you a failing grade. Contrary to popular opinion, most teachers do not enjoy failing students. However, because few students have the self-discipline and motivation to learn course material without external pressure, most instructors use tests and examinations to get students to study. But it is the student, not the instructor, who is responsible for doing the assignments.

Tests give you an insight into what your instructors consider important. They also provide you with a measure of your academic strengths and weaknesses. By reviewing your mistakes, you can devise a plan of study that will reduce or eliminate errors in future tests. Furthermore, tests afford you an opportunity to publicly demonstrate your ability to understand large volumes of material.

In summary, tests and examinations comprise one of the most important learning processes in your life. Preparing for and taking them involve scheduling your time, interpreting data, and sorting out essential and nonessential ideas. Without a doubt, whether or not you admit it, a well-designed test is a mind-expander.

GETTING READY

The most helpful review for tests starts with the first class assignment and continues routinely throughout the semester or quarter. There is no such thing as reviewing too early, but you can review too late. The primary demand made by a test or examination is to recall large amounts of data which are best learned in small doses. All-day or all-night study sessions generally result in mental and physical exhaustion. In most instances, cramming results in retaining only a small amount of information for a short time. Before you start a review, find out what the exam will cover and what kind it will be, e.g. objective, essay, combination. Below are some *pre-review* suggestions.

1. *Learn to pick out the most important course material.* Examples of typical important items are: theories and facts, vocabularies, general principles, rules, formulas, experimental conclusions, and historical sequences. You must be able to differentiate between fact and opinion. It is also wise for you to give attention to material emphasized by italics, boldface, question marks, and summary paragraphs.

2. *Make up your own questions to predict test questions.* This requires that you understand how your instructor thinks and what he or she considers important. Do not try to create easy questions; they are seldom the ones that will be on the test.

3. *Review and, if necessary, reorganize your course notes.* Try to divide your notes into units that are easy to remember. For example, in mathematics your notes can be divided into: redefinitions, word problems, theorems, formulas, and general concepts.

4. *Read end of chapter questions.* These exercises will get you into the process of responding to course-related questions. Know what your instructor expects when the question says: define, explain, diagram, illustrate, compare and contrast, describe, interpret, and enumerate.

5. *Review your most difficult subjects first.* This will relieve your mind so that you do not feel anxious when reviewing less difficult subjects.

6. *Ask for help before the examination.* If you wait until the examination has begun before you ask your instructor or a classmate for help, it is too late—you will probably fail. There is ample time before each examination to get help with course material.

7. *Remember that passing an examination should be the result of skill, not luck.* If you do your studying correctly, your grades will not be accidental or a matter of luck. The odds are against students who guess the answers to exam questions.

8. *Make sure you know where the examination is to be taken, when it is to be taken, and what you are expected and allowed to bring.* Get there early and with the appropriate materials.

Because forgetting occurs quickly after lectures, you should begin the review immediately after each lecture. It is advisable to spread your review times so that no single review becomes psychologically unnerving and physically draining. The sheer amount of material covered in most mid-term and final examinations often leads to procrastination. The all too common pre-test cramming sessions will tire you so much that you will not be alert during the test. Below is a summary of proven review principles.

1. *Spaced review periods are more effective than one concentrated*

review. Properly spaced time intervals will allow you to assimilate and organize course materials.

2. *Draft a fairly rigid review schedule.* By making out your schedule in advance and following it, you will be able to see your progress. This will also help to prevent procrastination.

3. *Study alone for the major portion of your review.* Studying with other persons can result in focusing only on materials they are uncertain about. If you must study with someone, carefully select your topics and study mates.

4. *Understand what you are studying.* Only by understanding what you are studying will you do more than resort to sheer memorization. You should strive to learn the material.

5. *Study selectively.* You have a limited amount of review time and it can be used best by determining what are the highlights of the topics under review.

6. *Read selectively.* Read only the portions of material which are vague in your mind or information which needs reinforcement by additional reading. Do not reread every word.

7. *During the review, maintain your usual eating, sleeping, and exercise habits.* Disturbance of these habits will result in confusion and fatigue.

8. *Cut back on your recreational activities and keep them to a reasonable minimum.* It is not wise to eliminate recreation, but it can be reduced during this period.

All methods of study are based on three basic skills of learning: (1) finding out what you want, (2) setting it in your mind, and (3) applying a method to allow you to learn it. There are several mechanical approaches to study, and we will discuss two of them: the SQ3R method of study and the 4S = M formula. We encourage you to seek out other methods and try them, too. You may prefer to mix methods. All good methods will include reading, questioning, and reciting. One method of study might prove excellent for one course but poor for another. In summary, select methods that fit you and your courses.

Reading and Studying

Most students erroneously believe that reading and studying are identical processes. It is true that reading is an important part of studying, but reading and studying are two different processes. *Reading* is a mental process used to *understand* written information, while *studying* is a process used to *remember* and *recall* it. Many students also believe that the best way to remember information is to read every word over and over again.

The best reading and studying methods for you are the ones that help you. If the suggestions in this book help you, use them. If they do not, devise your own study system. (See references at the end of this book.) Ideally, you will read course materials before studying them. Admittedly, there is a thin line between reading and studying. The line may be less blurred if you think of underlining as the beginning of studying. That is, you must first read the material before you decide what to underline for future reference. The procedures for reading and studying are:

1. Preview the chapters.
2. Skim and scan all sections of chapters.
3. Underline or highlight relevant portions.
4. Make notes for studying.
5. Recite the information you want to learn.

The good reader has three main objectives: (1) to concentrate on the material being read, (2) to remember as much as possible, and (3) to associate or apply what he or she reads to personal experiences. The good reader is able to read everything or skim it, depending on the nature of the work and what is desired. No matter whether you are reading comprehensively or skimming, you should:

• Know the purpose for which you are reading.
• Expect to remember what you read.
• Read for ideas—not words.
• Summarize what you read in your own words.

Improvement in reading and studying is only likely to occur by planning. If you have bad reading and study habits, they tend to be corrected only after a long period of practice. Initially, there will be a period of frustration. Practice for improvement in reading, for example, begins with the first sentence and ends with the last chapter. Learning is a process of progressive mastery. Once you start practicing for improvement, try to not go back to the old habits.

PREVIEW THE CHAPTERS

Typically, when assigned a book to read, students turn to the first page of Chapter One and begin reading. They not only skip many important portions of the book but also begin the intensive reading process too soon. *Previewing* is a process used to understand how the various parts of a chapter interrelate and what constitutes the total "inner stuff" of each chapter. A preview includes quickly examining introductory paragraphs, headings, illustrations, tables, figures, and other features of a chapter. It takes time to preview a book, but it is time well spent. Before you preview a chapter, you should familiarize yourself with the:

- Title.
- Front and back cover information.
- Author's biographical data, if available.
- Publication date.
- Table of Contents.
- Preface or Introduction.
- Appendix.
- Glossary.
- Index.
- Bibliography or References.

The *table of contents* provides an overview of the major topics discussed in the book. Immediately after the table of contents is an *introduction* or *preface*—some books have both. Here you will find the author's reason for writing the book as well as his or her philosophy pertaining to the subjects in the book. If there is supplementary material, it is placed in the *appendix*, which is usually placed after the glossary or, if none is included, the last chapter. Questionnaires, laws, and letters are examples of material found in appendixes. A *glossary* is an alphabetical list of terms and definitions. Some tests include short glossaries in the main body of the text. You may also find a *bibliography* or *references* at the back of the book or at the end of each chapter. This is a valuable source of where to go for more details about topics covered in the textbook.

After you have skimmed the introductory and summary portions of the book, you are ready to preview the chapter. Previewing consists of reading:

- Lists at the beginning or end of the chapter.
- Introduction at the beginning of the chapter.
- Summary at the end of the chapter.
- Headings (major and subtopic) within the chapter.
- Figures, tables, and drawings.

Some books begin or end with learning objectives or questions under headings such as "Learning Objectives," "Learning Goals," "Objectives," "Goals," "Performance Objectives," or "Study Guides." These lists will give a clue to the points that are most important in the chapter. If questions or exercises are in the chapter, read them before you read the chapter—even if they are at the end of the chapter. This will help you to read for specific content. Some books include lists of terms important to understanding the chapters. Copy the terms in your notebook and use them for review.

The first paragraphs of a chapter usually contain the key units of thought that make up the chapter. The poor reader counts the pages and worries about the amount of time required to do the reading; the good reader finds the units of thought upon which the paragraphs are built. If you read words or pages only because they are assigned, and are merely trying to finish the task, you will do just that—read pages without comprehension.

Headings often tell you what topics are to be discussed. Many textbooks have more than two types of headings, and generally:

1. If headings are printed in different sizes of type, the larger the type, the more important the heading.
2. If several headings are printed in the same type but some are printed in black ink and others are printed in another color, the non-black headings are more important.
3. If headings are the same size type but some are in boldface and others are in italics, the boldface headings are more important.
4. If all headings are the same size but some are printed in all capital letters and others are not, the headings printed in all capital letters are more important.

Graphic materials summarize data and sentiments. Labels and titles of illustration help you to identify their components. Remember that illustrations are not given to distract, confuse, or mislead you. Find out what the author is trying to tell you.

After previewing a textbook or chapter, you should know (1) what the material is mainly about, (2) how it is organized, and (3) how difficult it is.

SKIMMING AND SCANNING

Learning to skim and scan textbooks will help you to study materials that are difficult for you to understand. *Skimming* involves searching for main ideas by reading introductory paragraphs, topic headings, and other organizational cues such as summaries. *Scanning* involves looking for specific facts or key words. Skimming and scanning are the careful previewing of a chapter before reading and underlining it. Skimming and scanning are especially valuable skills for studying scientific textbooks. Most science textbooks are well organized with main topics and subtopics clearly delineated. They also contain helpful illustrations, terminology lists, and explicit summaries. Even so, some students are intimidated by the materials and tend to ignore these cues as they plod through the chapters word by word, trying to memorize it all. This, of course, is impossible if you do not have a photographic memory.

Unless you are able to understand thoroughly the major ideas and concepts the author presents, you will find yourself trying unsuccessfully to cram isolated data into your memory. It will literally go in your eyes and out your head like water runs through a sieve. What little information you retain will hardly allow you to excel in your course. It is important that you do preliminary skimming to get hold of the main topics for study. By scanning the chapter, you can quickly locate new terms that you must understand in order to follow the author's reasoning. If you find words that you do not know but do not find definitions of these words in the chapter, you can look for definitions in other parts of the book or in other reference materials. In summary, skimming and scanning includes:

- Dividing chapters into sections.
- Reading introductory paragraphs for each section.
- Reading headings.
- Reading words printed in special type, e.g., italics and boldface.
- Interpreting tables, graphs, and diagrams.

The additional time it takes to skim and scan your books will shorten the time it takes you to learn the information contained in them. This may be hard for you to grasp, but you have to spend time in order to save time studying.

UNDERLINING AND HIGHLIGHTING

Skillfully and purposefully marking your textbooks is much more useful than taking chapter notes. You will retain more by marking your textbooks than any other study method. A well-marked chapter can be reviewed in considerably less time than it would take to re-read a book. Once marked, the main points and relationships between ideas will be easily discernible (see Figure 7). You will only need to read the unmarked material if you cannot recall the meaning of the marked passages.

Underlining may be done with a pencil, but it is usually done with a ballpoint pen. Most students need a straight-edged instrument to assist them in making neat lines. Highlighting does not require anything except felt-tipped pens that contain water-colored ink, usually yellow. Whatever method of marking is used, it should be used consistently. There are several guidelines for marking a book, including the following.

1. Wait until *after* you have read a chapter or a significant part of it before you mark it, and mark only the things you want to *learn*.
2. Mark the *main points*. If necessary, write letters, Roman numerals, or numbers in the margin to note the order of the ideas.
3. Mark not only the main ideas but also note the relationship between them. You may also want to circle key words or draw arrows to connect them.

4. If you believe it is important to mark subordinate points, do so judiciously. Mark the minimum number of subordinate ideas.

<u>PREADDICTION</u>. The road to alcoholism begins when drinking is no longer social but a means of psychological escape from tensions and inhibitions. Initially, this type of drinker is in reasonable control. However, heavy drinkers begin to fall into a definite pattern:

①*Gross drinking behavior*: They begin to drink more heavily and more often than their friends. "Getting high" becomes a habit. When drunk, they may develop a "big shot" complex, recklessly (Ex) spending money and boasting of real and imagined accomplishments.

②*Blackouts*: A "blackout," or temporary loss of memory, is not to be confused with "passing out," which is a loss of consciousness. Drinkers suffering from a blackout <u>cannot remember</u> things they said, things they did, or places they visited. It is important to note that even a social drinker can have a blackout. With prospective alcoholics, blackouts are more frequent and develop into a pattern.

Important

③*Gulping and sneaking drinks*: Anxious to maintain a euphoric level, they begin to drink heavily at parties and slyly gulp (Ex) down extra ones when they think nobody is looking. They also may "fortify" themselves before going to a party to help along their euphoria. Ultimately, they begin to feel guilty about this behavior and avoid talking about alcohol or drinking.

④*Chronic hangovers*: As they become more and more reliant on alcohol as a stress reliever, "morning after" hangovers become more frequent and increasingly painful.

<u>ADDICTION</u>. Until now, the problem drinker has been drinking heavily but not always conspicuously. More importantly, he or she <u>has been able to stop drinking, but not now</u>. At this point, he or she develops the symptoms of addiction with increased rapidity.

①*Loss of control*: This is the problem drinkers' most common sign that their habit has become an addiction. They still may refuse to accept a drink, but once they take one they <u>cannot stop</u>. A single drink is likely to trigger a chain reaction that will continue without a break until a state of complete intoxication is achieved.

Important

②*The alibi system*: Their loss of control induces feelings of guilt and shame, so they utilize an elaborate system of "reasons"

** This is likely to be on the test **

Figure 7. Marked book page.

5. Use a *variety* of marks, and use them consistently. For example, you may want to underline main ideas, circle important names and dates, and use a felt pen to note key paragraphs. You may want to write question marks in the margin before statements you do not understand.
6. Summary words or phrases written in the margin, or at the top or bottom of pages, should be used sparingly and, when possible, use abbreviations.
7. Write formulas and terminology on the inside front and back covers.
8. Whatever system you use, *do not overdo it.* Keep your marks few and simple. If most of a page is marked, it is the same as if nothing were marked.
9. Review your markings immediately after you finish an assignment.
10. If you mark your book and still feel the need to make notes, base them on your testbook markings.

Some students elect not to mark books so that they can sell them back to a bookstore. This is not a wise savings. It is better to keep a book for reference than to save on its actual cost by reselling it. A well stocked personal library is invaluable in the world of work and the foundation for leisure-time reading. If for no other reason, keep your books as mementos of your college days.

MAKING NOTES FOR STUDYING

Notes made from books should be written on index cards or notebook paper. There are three reasons for you to make notes if marking your books is not sufficient for you to learn the material:

1. When you write notes, you process the information both visually and mentally. Some students learn information simultaneously while writing notes.
2. Written notes reduce the amount of information to be learned. Several note cards or note pages are less frightening than hundreds of pages of a textbook.
3. Textbooks are organized to make information *understandable*, while notes are organized to make the information *easier for you to learn.*

Most students write notes on notebook paper rather than on cards. Cards have several advantages over notebook paper. They make it easier to separate what has been learned from what has not been learned. They are more convenient to carry and study during brief free periods. They increase the likelihood that you will learn the material rather than merely read it. Whether you use cards or notebook paper, the following guidelines are offered.

- Write titles that describe what you want to learn on each note. Usually this is written on the opposite side of the note.
- List pertinent information about each topic.
- Include examples that will aid in understanding the terms and concepts.
- If the information is written on more than one page or card, number the notes.

RECITING TO LEARN

Most of the information you must learn can be learned by repeating it silently or aloud. The greatest proportion of your study time should be

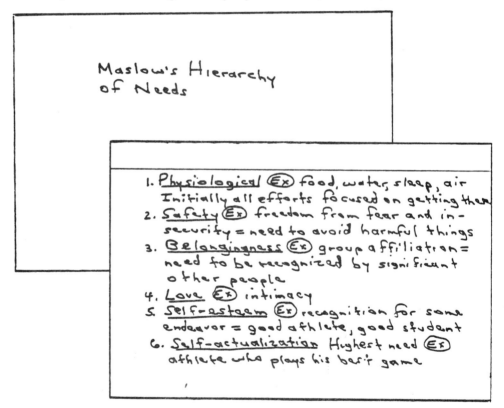

Figure 8. Note card.

recitation. This is precompetition practice. Obviously, you must decide what is important to learn. Trying to predict questions that will be in an examination is an effective study aid. When predicting questions, you are likely to learn the answers not by rote memory, but with understanding. By giving answers to your questions, you prepare for the examination. Reciting alone is effective, but you may learn more and quicker in group study sessions.

Demonstrating your knowledge of the course material in group sessions does several things: (1) It motivates you to know the material before the group meets. (2) It enables you to get feedback. (3) Your self-confidence is reinforced as you master the material and get positive feedback. (4) It allows you to fill in gaps in your own knowledge. (5) You get additional perspectives of the problems and material. Even so, group study sessions are only as effective as the team members. Poorly constituted groups merely waste the time of the participants.

PUTTING IT TOGETHER: SQ3R

The Survey Q Three R (SQ3R) method of study outlines in concrete form the techniques we have been discussing. Indeed, the SQ3R method is a proven, useful method of study which can guide you through a course in such a way that you discover the important facts and ideas contained in reading assignments. The end result is that SQ3R can help you to master and retain course materials. The five steps of SQ3R are: (1) survey, (2) question, (3) read, (4) recite, and (5) review.

Survey

Skim and scan the reading assignment, taking no more than five minutes to preview an entire chapter. Check the headings and subheadings because they are the author's outline and make it easy for you to follow his or her ideas. Inspect all illustrations because they summarize in visible and tangible ways facts and ideas contained in the text. Read the introductory and summary paragraphs because they contain important points and concepts for you to understand. A survey of this nature will familiarize you with the chapter before you study it in greater detail.

Question

Ask yourself the following question: "What are the most important points?" This will allow you to convert headings and subheadings into who, what, why, when, and how questions about the reading material. It is imperative that you challenge yourself to find answers to these questions.

TABLE 7-1

Study Systems

Texts		Lectures
1. Know purpose of reading	**P**	1. Review previous lectures
2. Know relation of chapters to text	**R**	2. Skim reading assignments
3. Understand structure of chapters	**E**	
4. Acknowledge reading difficulty level for you	**V**	
5. Note new vocabulary	**I**	
6. Study graphics	**E**	
7. Break chapters into workable parts	**W**	
1. Keep purpose in mind	**R**	1. Pay attention
2. Ask questions about information	**E**	2. Attend to structure and information, not
3. Note main ideas, details, trivia	**A**	emotions
4. Note function of information	**D**	3. Write down relevant examples
5. Attend to key words		4. Translate into your own words
6. Set time goals	**&**	5. Be consistent in form, abbreviations, etc.
7. Lightly check in pencil ideas appearing to		6. Check with instructor or friends on vocabu-
be important	**R**	lary or ideas missed
	E	7. Copy missed notes from two persons, not
	C	just one
	O	
	R	
	D	
1. Summarize periodically	**R**	1. Edit with outline and questions
2. Notemaking—make permanent those checks	**E**	2. Fill in missing points
that are really necessary; include questions	**C**	3. Correlate with text
3. Reflect on possible uses; differences between	**A**	4. Recite by answering questions
text and class	**L**	5. Record important words, ideas on cards
4. Review previous material before reading next	**L**	6. Write down reflections
chapter		7. Review previous lectures

Read

Read the assignment carefully and actively. Knowledge will not pass by osmosis or magic from the page of a book to your brain as a result of reading it. You must pursue your reading aggressively. Underline or highlight key words and phrases to aid you in learning and recalling major points. Use symbols—asterisks, question marks, or exclamation points—to indicate important data or ideas. Divide the material into small sections, rather than long, nonstop reading periods. Summarize key ideas in your own words in the page margins.

Recite

Stop at intervals to recite from memory the main points of the assignment. Look away from the book and ask yourself questions you have already made up. If you cannot do this immediately after reading the material, you are not likely to do it at a later date. Forty to fifty percent of the material you read is forgotten within 15 to 30 minutes after you read it. Thus, immediate recall is an essential first step toward continued retention of course material.

Review

Review the material at periodic intervals. This will refresh your memory and freeze in your memory the important information. If you wait until just before an examination for a review, it probably will be too late. That is a good time for the last review, but not the first one. Your understanding of the material should increase with each review. Reviewing is nothing more than going over the material again and again until you know it.

You should repeat steps *question, read, recite,* and *review* as you tackle each succeeding section of written material. This is not an easy way to study but it is an efficient technique. It will require continuous deliberate effort on your part if you are to master this method of study. Furthermore, you must constantly resist passive habits of reading. Listed below are errors some students make while using the SQ3R study method. Check all the ones that apply to you—even if you don't use the SQ3R method.

- ☐ 1. *Failing to turn topic headings into questions.* Many students ignore topic headings, or overlook them.
- ☐ 2. *Making notes in too much detail.* Too much information is the same as too little—it impedes learning.
- ☐ 3. *Failing to use notes for review.* It is a waste of your time and energy to make notes if you don't use them.
- ☐ 4. *Depending exclusively on underlining or highlighting material.* The material you mark must be reviewed if you want to learn it.
- ☐ 5. *Believing that the SQ3R method takes too much time.* The time spent learning the method is a small amount of time compared to the time compared to the time you will have to spend rereading course materials.

4S = M FORMULA

The 4S = M formula means Four Steps = Mastery, and the four steps are: (1) the preliminary survey, (2) reading the assignment for ideas and converting portions into questions, (3) the quick review—rereading important portions you do not recall at a quick glance, and (4) summarizing the material briefly and logically.

The *preliminary survey* is skimming and scanning as discussed in the SQ3R method of study.

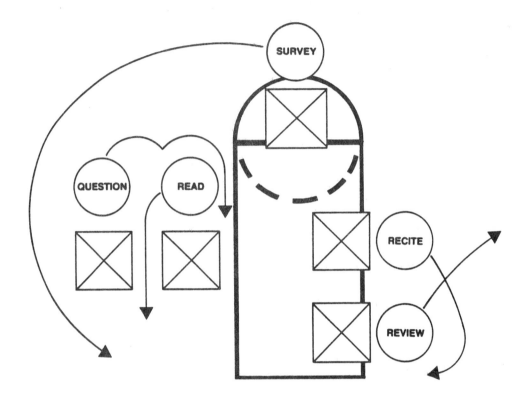

Figure 9. Basic study moves.

Reading the assignment for ideas and converting small units into questions is based on three words: (1) reading, (2) ideas, and (3) questions. Reading means concentrating, remembering, and applying information. This is intensive reading—reading to understand clearly and to apply the knowledge. Reading for ideas requires you to see groups of words rather than single words. Reading for ideas will naturally lead you to questions that each idea fosters. It is the formation of questions that gives the most impetus for the mind to grasp the material.

The *quick review* step is not only a check against incomplete preparation but also can increase your speed in reading, recall, and comprehension. Skimming is the method of reading used for quick reviews. But once missing parts are located, you should return to intensive reading.

The fourth step, *summarizing the material briefly and logically,* is oral. If you can do this successfully, you will know: (1) what the assignment entails, (2) the order in which it moves, (3) key ideas, and (4) what the assignment was designed to teach.

Whatever method of study you use, select one that will help you to: (1) learn efficiently, (2) understand course material, (3) retard forgetting, and (4) apply concepts learned in one course to another. Learning a new study technique, like learning any new skill, is likely to go slowly at first. As you become more proficient, you will be able to progress more quickly. Familiarity and experience will make your method more effective. Remember, study methods that are most helpful to you may also be the most difficult for you to apply consistently, just as more intricate skills are the most difficult to learn to apply.

Good methods of study will eventually shorten the time you need for study, and you will accomplish more in less time than required for a poor method of study. Remember, however, that all reading is not study. Nor is staring at the pages of a book necessarily reading. You must want to read and study.

REMEMBERING

A considerable amount of information is known about the learning process, but behavioral scientists do not fully understand how memory works. Experimentally, it can be proven that physical traces of what we experience remain with us. Psychologists have electrically stimulated certain areas of subjects' brains and reproduced in their consciousness a vivid flashback of sounds, smells, and sights of events that had been repressed for several years. From these experiments have come the theory that we never actually lose what we experience. It is stored in our computer (the mind) and can be retrieved with proper methods of recall.

You will remember material more easily if you understand it. This chapter has provided several methods to help you understand course materials by organizing the details and their relationships to each other. If course materials make sense to you, the various parts will be easier to recall. For example, medical students who have to remember the bones that make up the skeleton will remember them more easily if they know the function of each bone and how it interacts with the others. History students who have to remember names, dates, and details of an historical period will remember them if they understand the overriding social trends and philosophies of the time. In other words, you are likely to remember course assignments when they are placed in context of important ideas, principles, and theories. This is really the SQ3R method of study—survey, question, read, recite, and review. The more thoroughly and deeply you get into course assignments, the more you will remember. Because knowledge is cumulative, the more pieces you understand, the less threatened you will be by the total picture.

The key to recall is to get beyond the recognition stage. That is, you must make a conscious effort to learn what you read. If it is hard for you to remember the material, it may be because you do not have a desire or interest to remember it. Or, it may be hard to remember because you did not read it with the intent to remember it. You must have a reason to remember. Talk with the instructor or students who seem to be interested in the course and find out what motivates them. Read with the intent to remember—hold yourself responsible for information which must be remembered. Make every reading count.

In certain courses (e.g. foreign languages, sciences, or mathematics) you may have to *overlearn* the material. Overlearning is practice well beyond the point of initial mastery. It is the process of recall of information to the point where conscious effort is no longer needed. This is how most children learn the alphabet and to tell time on nondigital clocks. Overlearning is accelerated when we have sight, sound, and feeling to help us. If we can write it down, say it aloud, and touch it, we tend to learn it more quickly.

FINAL CHECK

Before we discuss specific strategies for passing tests and writing papers, let us briefly review the process of successful study. Check each tip that you want to remember.

1. **The Job of Learning**
   ☐ Learning means work.
   ☐ Being a student is not an easy job.
   ☐ Three hours in a class means at least 4-6 hours of out-of-class study.
   ☐ There is something important to be learned in every class.
2. **What to Do**
   ☐ Get organized.
   ☐ Budget your time wisely.
   ☐ Find interest in each class.
   ☐ Make time to study.
   ☐ Do not get too comfortable.
   ☐ Avoid disturbances when studying.
   ☐ Do not cram for classes.
   ☐ Get notebooks for every class.
   ☐ Strive for the highest grades.
   ☐ Make use of time between classes.
   ☐ Study your hardest subjects when you are most alert.
   ☐ Do not be afraid to accept responsibility.

3. **Classes**
   ☐ Read lessons before they are discussed in class.
   ☐ Listen to what the instructor says.
   ☐ Think about what you hear.
   ☐ Critically evaluate what the instructor says.
   ☐ Ask questions if you do not understand portions of a lecture.
   ☐ Take part in class discussions.
   ☐ Make systematic notes.
   ☐ Re-read your notes shortly after each class and make necessary corrections.
4. **The Textbook**
   ☐ Read the title of the book and name of the author.
   ☐ Find out who published the book and its latest copyright date.
   ☐ Read the preface, skim the table of contents, appendix, and index.
5. **The Chapter**
   ☐ Read the introduction at the beginning of the chapter and summary at the end of the chapter.
   ☐ Read the headings and subheadings.
   ☐ Make questions from headings. Your questions should cover:
   - Definitions
   - Words and phrases in italics or boldface print
   - Authors and their work
   - Individuals and their theories or accomplishments
   - List, categories, and classifications
   ☐ Read the chapter section by section, actively searching for answers to your questions.
   ☐ Underline or highlight important ideas.
   ☐ Make notes in the margin.
   ☐ At the end of the chapter, look away from the book and recite the answers to your questions.

Chapter 8

PASSING TESTS

Some students think of tests as obstacle courses to be avoided, or as personal wars between themselves and their instructors. Other students see tests as the ultimate academic punishment. All of these beliefs are based on fear, which can render students ineffective during examinations. There are some instances when you might reasonably expect disastrous results after taking tests. Examples of these instances are: (1) when you have not learned the material, (2) when you are overly tired, and (3) when your previous test scores were so low that you must earn an "A" or "B" in order to get a final grade of "D." Put a check in the box in front of the statements below that describe your test-taking behaviors.

- ☐ You consistently score lower on tests than on daily recitations.
- ☐ You almost always find fault with your tests—they are too long, questions too vague, or the material you studied is not included.
- ☐ You frequently complain about your instructors.
- ☐ You lose sleep before examinations and are fatigued when you take them.
- ☐ You almost always study for tests with classmates whose subject knowledge is less than your own.
- ☐ You cannot find important notes when they are needed for review.
- ☐ You have a mental block when you enter the test room.
- ☐ You finish the test before most students taking it, feel confident you have done well, but score low.
- ☐ You take too much time answering each question.
- ☐ You frequently encounter questions that you believe have two correct answers, so you guess which one to choose.

If you checked three or more of the behaviors listed above, you have negative study habits that require immediate attention. One of the first steps to take is to accept tests and examinations as vital, nondamaging aspects of your academic growth and development. It is normal to be anxious prior to academic competition, but it is not normal to be immobilized by the thought of it.

A GENERAL APPROACH

Students who are high achievers in college not only use effective study methods but they also use effective test-taking methods. Studying is the practice before academic competition, while writing papers and taking tests are aspects of the competitive game. Unlike athletes who may do poorly in practice but excel in competition, there are few students who do poorly when they study but excel when taking tests. In academics, practice almost always pays off, while failure to study or using poor study habits almost always leads to low grades. A proven general approach to test-taking includes the following.

1. Minimize your test anxiety.
2. Skim tests and allocate your time.
3. Read the directions carefully and follow them.
4. Answer the easiest questions first.
5. Unless told otherwise, answer all the questions.
6. Check your answers carefully before turning in the examination.
7. Ignore other students taking the test.

You should read the questions carefully. Do not rush. Just as reading textbooks, you should take time to see all the words in an examination. If you rush headlong into the exam, you are likely to overlook or misread key words or phrases. When you choose a correct answer, look at the other options and be satisfied that it is correct or true in every aspect. It is helpful to reason out an answer: Does it make sense? Do not be afraid to begin your analysis with the facts you know. A closer look at the general approach listed above will give you a better understanding of tests and how to pass them.

Minimize Test Anxiety

Text anxiety is an uneasiness you experience because of fear that you might fail or do poorly answering the questions. Physical symptoms of test anxiety include rapid heartbeat, sweating, headaches, diarrhea, and shortness of breath. In extreme cases, you will not be able to eat or sleep. Sometimes your mind will appear to go blank. Seldom will any of this cause you to "go crazy." You may do some irrational things, but you are not likely to become mentally ill. Individuals who are unprepared to take a test usually behave much differently than they would if they were test-wise. Merely using good test procedures can reduce your anxiety. But procedures alone will not compensate for inadequate study.

It is important that you eat and sleep well before taking tests. A nourished and well rested person is able to adjust to a mentally grueling test. On the other hand, if your mind and body are stressed, the test results will almost always be less than you desire. As in most competitive activities, you must get the body ready before you tax your mind. And you must relax before the test. The following exercises will help you to relax:

1. Without smiling so that it shows, relax your face and smile on the inside.
2. Take a deep breath—one that seems to go to the bottom of your feet. Hold your breath.
3. Then quietly, smiling inside, let your breath out as slowly as you can.

Do not worry about what onlookers say or think as you try to relieve your anxiety. It will be you, not them, who fail if you cannot relieve the anxiety. Once you get over the fear of taking tests, you will find the higher grades you earn worth the few snickers you may receive while doing the exercises. See Table 8-1 for tension relaxation exercises that focus on specific muscle areas.

If you try these exercises but cannot relax during tests, get professional help to overcome test anxiety. Some colleges offer relaxation courses, others have counselors or medical personnel to assist students who have disabling test anxiety. Before you seek professional help, however, make sure that the tension is due to a fear of taking tests and not because you have failed to adequately prepare for the tests. You will do poorly whether or not you are relaxed if you do not know the material.

Skim and Allocate Your Time

Do not answer a single question before you skim a test. Find out what you are going to face—how many questions, what kind of questions, and how many points are given for each question. By observing the point value of the questions, you will be able to figure out how to best spend your time. For example, you may discover that you need to answer 50 questions worth a total of 100 points: 25 multiple choice (1 point each question), 10 true or false (2 points each), 10 matching (1 point each), and 5 short essay (9 points each). Because the essay questions comprise 45 percent of the points, you should spend roughly 45 percent of your time on these questions. The multiple choice questions comprise 25 percent of the points, true or false comprise 20 percent, and matching comprise 10 percent. You should allocate your time accordingly.

TABLE 8-1

Relaxation Exercises

The following relaxation exercises are designed for a sitting position. Therefore, you can easily do them while sitting in a classroom. In order to be optimally effective, you should try to determine the location of your tension.

Tension Location	Exercise
The back of the hands and wrists	Clench your fists—tighter-relax
The bicep muscles	Clench your fists (feel the bicep tighten)—tighter—relax
The upper portion of the forearm	Holding both arms straight out, stretch—tighter—relax
The entire forehead	Wrinkle your forehead and lift your eyebrows upward—tighter—relax
The eyelids	Close your eyes—tighter—relax
The area around the tongue	Bring your tongue to the roof of your mouth, press—tighter—relax
The jaws	Clench your jaws—tighter—relax
The region around the mouth	Press your lips together—tighter—relax
The muscles at the back of the neck	Press head backward, roll your head to side front and side back—relax
The muscles at the front of the neck and jaws	Bend head forward, press chin to chest—straighter—relax
The muscles of the shoulders and lower neck	Bring shoulders up to ears, move around—relax
The chest area	Take a deep breath—hold it for 5 seconds, exhale slowly—relax
The abdominal region	Tighten stomach muscles—relax
The lower back	Pull shoulders back—arch back—relax
The thigh muscles	Press heels down hard—harder—relax
The calf muscles	Point toes away from face—relax Point toes toward face—relax

Throughout these exercises, pay special attention to your breathing—it should be easy in, easy out. Once you are in control of yourself, you will be able to get control over your test-taking.

Read Directions and Follow Them

There is a tendency for students to lose points on examinations because they did not read carefully the directions and follow them. It is especially painful if you know the answers but lose points because of false assumptions about what you were asked to do. It may seem unimportant in what form you must give the answers, but it is very important to people who grade tests.

This is not unique to classroom competition. Every sport has specific rules regarding the acceptable ways to score points. It is foolish to lose points or to be disqualified for rule violations or not following directions.

Answer the Easiest Questions First

Most tests require that you finish within a comparatively short period of time. This is another way of saying that you seldom have all the time you would like. Therefore, the major objective is to wisely use your time. For this reason, we recommend that you answer the easiest questions first. (If none are easy, you are in trouble!) There are no exceptions to this rule. You should answer the easiest questions first no matter what kind of test you are taking. There are four reasons this is the best test strategy.

1. You are most likely to answer correctly the easiest questions. This will minimize your loss of points if you run out of time before answering all questions.
2. You reduce test anxiety by getting a few questions answered. The longer you ponder a question, the more internal pressure you will feel and, relatedly, the more self-doubt you will have. The easy questions are confidence builders.
3. Sometimes answers to one or two questions can help you recall answers to other questions. Seldom are the questions unrelated. Thus, the process of answering the easy questions first is similar to putting together a crossword puzzle—slowly the total picture takes form.

TABLE 8-2
Directions Exercise

Read these directions carefully. You have 2 minutes to complete the exercise. Get a pencil or pen and a blank sheet of paper. When you have finished, ask a friend to check your answers. Read all the following directions before beginning.

---

1. Print your name in the upper right-hand corner of the paper.
   Print your last name first.
2. Draw five circles in the center of the paper, and then draw a circle around your circles.
3. Print your first name backwards in the upper left-hand side of the page.
4. Draw a picture of a flower in the bottom right-hand corner of the paper.
5. Write your age on the paper. Subtract 10 and divide by 2. Multiply your total by 3.
6. Draw a diagonal line from the lower left-hand edge of the paper to the top right-hand edge of the paper.
7. Now that you have read all the directions, do number 3.

How well did you follow the instructions?

---

4. Even if the questions are unrelated, answering one may refresh your memory of another. This is sometimes referred to as *free association*. Of course, you have to trust yourself enough to accept answers when they "pop" into your mind. Actually, answers seldom pop, they flow through recall.

If you are not relaxed and self-confident, answers to difficult questions will come and go without you recognizing them. If you are unable to answer a question after reading it twice, move on to the next question. Continue this process until you have read each question twice and answered as many as you can. Repeat this process as many times as you can before you have to start guessing. Budget your time carefully.

Unless Told Otherwise, Answer All the Questions

Most test grades are based on the total number of correct answers. If there is a penalty for guessing, it will be part of the directions. Where there is no penalty for guessing, answer all questions. If you do not answer a question, you guarantee yourself no credit for it, while you may increase your score by guessing at answers.

Check Your Answers Carefully Before Turning in the Examination

One careless answer can be the difference between an A or B grade, while several careless answers can be the difference between passing and failing. A word of caution is in order: In most instances, your first answer is correct. This is especially true for multiple-choice, true-false, matching, and fill-in questions. Therefore, you should change an answer only when you feel reasonably sure it is incorrect.

Ignore Other Students Taking the Test

Do not race with other students to finish the test. The quickest students are not always the highest scoring students. In fact, a large percentage of low-scoring students finish tests early. Worry about how you use your time, not how fast or slow other people are when they take tests. You are only responsible for yourself.

TABLE 8-3

Self-Talk and Test Taking

Anxiety producing self-talk and test-relevant self-talk are mutually incompatible. When you engage in one process, you prevent the other from occurring. Below are some examples of helpful and unhelpful examples of self-talk.

Behavior	Unhelpful Self-Talk	Helpful Self-Talk
Worrying about your performance, including how well other students are doing compared with you.	"He's not through yet—good! . . . She finished early. . . . I hope I'm not the last one to finish."	"They finished early, I wonder . . . there's no way I can know how well they've done."
Pondering too long over alternative answers or responses.	"I must get the other questions right. Why is this question taking me so long?"	"I'm making too much of the questions. I'll give what I think are the best answers."
Being preoccupied with your bodily reactions to the test.	"Settle down and stop shaking . . . my hands are shaking. What's happening to me?"	"My hands are shaking . . . I'm tense . . . I've got to stop for a moment. Deep breath . . . calm . . . relax, that's better, this test won't kill me."
Worrying about doing poorly on a question.	"I'll never answer these questions. I'll never pass this course. I'm going to flunk out."	"I don't remember how to do this! I'd better move on. . . . I can get more points if I don't panic."
Thoughts or feelings of inadequacy—self-criticism or self-condemnation, calling yourself "stupid."	"That's two in a row I don't know. Why didn't I remember the answers? I'm so dumb. I'll never learn this stuff."	"I should know that . . . Maybe it will come to me later . . . No need to get uptight. I'll take one question at a time."

Now it's your turn. Monitor your own self-talk and try to eliminate *unhelpful* self-talk.

MULTIPLE-CHOICE QUESTIONS

There are basically two kinds of multiple-choice questions: (1) questions followed by possible answers and (2) incomplete statements followed by possible missing words or sentences. In most instances, there are four options and you must select the correct response. In properly written questions, only one option is correct. The other responses contain a word or words that make them incorrect. Moving through a multiple-choice test is similar to moving through a minefield—all responses look correct, but if you select the wrong ones, your final score will wreck your grade-point average. So, move carefully through a test.

Watch Out for Sequences

What is the answer if a question asks for the correct sequence for human development and gives you the following choices?

a. Adolescence, early childhood, adulthood, prepuberty
b. Early childhood, adulthood, adolescence, prepuberty
c. Early childhood, prepuberty, adolescence, adulthood
d. Prepuberty, early childhood, adolescence, adulthood

The answer is c. Your lecture notes should have had the correct sequence. You should draw a line through the obviously incorrect answers (a and b) which do not have adulthood as the final stage of growth. This narrows the choice between c and d and, thus, greatly increases your chance to select the correct answer. Do not be misled by incorrect sequences.

Circle or Underline "Not," "Except," "Incorrect," and "False"

Certain words greatly restrict the range of responses. Highlight qualifying words. Unfortunately, many students read the questions as if these words were not used. When this happens, the correct response is likely to be rejected for the opposite response which, of course, is incorrect.

Select the Answers You Studied

Do not second guess your notes at this stage. Sometimes you will be tempted to believe that your notes and the textbook were wrong because they do not contain words and phrases that appear on the test. If you have made good notes and carefully reviewed the textbook, do not be misled by new ideas and concepts. Stay with your best prepared material. Or, stated another way, do not panic and abandon your academic game plan.

Beware of Absolute Statements

Whenever you encounter answers with words such as *all, none, every, always, never,* and *invariably,* look for possible exceptions. If you find exceptions that apply, the answer with the absolute statement is incorrect. Answers with words such as *often, seldom, many, some, most, frequently,* and *generally* are more likely to be used in true statements.

Note Insulting or Ridiculous Statements

Seldom are insulting or ridiculous statements correct. The reason is quite simple: It is neither morally nor academically correct to demean people, and ridiculous statements have no basis in science. For instance:

1. Blacks are disproportionately represented in some varsity sports such as football, basketball, track, and wrestling because
   a. they are built for sports and other ethnic groups are not.
   b. their long ape-like arms give them an advantage.
   c. they have more opportunities than other ethnic groups to excel in these sports.
   d. all black people are natural athletes.

Whenever your options are between insulting and noninsulting responses, select the noninsulting response. In the question above, the answer is c. But be careful with this kind of question. Do not assume insult or ridicule where it is not intended. That is, do not let your biases and prejudices negatively color a question or response. Stated another way, do not automatically assume racism or sexism if an instructor uses *boy* or *girl* or *he* in the questions, for example.

When you answer multiple-choice questions, make marks on your exam paper (unless told not to do so) so that you can single out questionable words, statements, and phrases. Asterisks, question marks, circles, underlining, and other marks can help you to sort out the correct answers. But use marks sparingly. Too many marks will only confuse you.

TRUE-FALSE QUESTIONS

True-false questions have only one correct answer. They cannot be both true and false. If they are, the question is invalid. Because it is easier to write true statements than it is to write false statements, assume that each question is true until you convince yourself otherwise. Here, too, absolute statements (always, never, etc.) are likely to be a clue that a question is false. In order for a statement to be true, all parts of it must be true. You should dissect each question into separate but interrelated parts and determine if each part is true. For example:

T F Martin Luther King, Jr. was a prominent civil rights leader and the first black American to win a Nobel Peace Prize.

The first part of the statement is true: Dr. King was a prominent civil rights leader. The second part of the statement is false: He was not the first black American to win a Nobel Peace Prize. Therefore, the statement is false. If you are not sure whether a statement is true or false, but it could be either true or false depending on interpretation, select an answer and write your reason after it. It may also help you to circle or underline words or phrases which you believe make the statement false. Some students try to second guess their instructors by finding a pattern to the answers (e.g., T, F, T, F . . . or T, T, F, T, T, F . . .) or a percentage of true/false (e.g., 50/50, 30/70). Do not gamble with your grade this way. Answer each question according to the best interpretation you can make. Forget about patterns and percentages. If you must gamble, do it outside of class.

MATCHING AND SENTENCE COMPLETION QUESTIONS

The most common matching questions consist of two lists of items and students must demonstrate that they know which items belong together. For example, one column might consist of musicians and the other column might be a list of songs. It is a good strategy to make as many correct matches as possible before you start guessing. When one column has more items than the other one, use the column with the most items as the starting point for making matches. Sentence completion questions are usually taken directly from a textbook. A common mistake that students make is to critique the statements and try to rewrite them. Your task is not to correct the grammar or the substance of the statements but, instead, to provide the missing word or words. Argue about the structure or relevance of the test after it is returned to you. Answer each question in terms of what you have read or heard in class.

Objective Test Checklist

☐ 1. Find out exactly how much time you have, and estimate the amount of time to be spent on each question.
☐ 2. Read directions and listen to verbal comments about directions.

☐ 3. Skim the whole examination before giving it a quick, thorough reading.
☐ 4. Answer all the questions you are sure of first.
☐ 5. When a paragraph is given, read it through. Do not skip from a sentence in the paragraph to the answers below.
☐ 6. In multiple-choice questions, first cross out the obviously incorrect answers, then make your choice from the remaining ones.
☐ 7. If you narrow your answer to two choices, it is usually better to guess than to not answer the question. Do not guess if there is a severe penalty for wrong answers.
☐ 8. In most instances, absolute words such as *never, always, none,* and *all* make a false statement.
☐ 9. When answering completion questions, try to insert the technical terms or key phrases exactly as they appear in the textbook.
☐ 10. Change an original answer only if you have a strong hunch it is wrong.

ESSAY QUESTIONS

Most essay questions are designed to evaluate your ability to make valid generalizations or apply broad principles and support your responses with sound evidence. In essence, essay test items provide instructors with insight into your grasp of course materials. Your grade is usually determined by (1) how much is written, (2) the accuracy of what you write, (3) spelling, grammar, and syntax, and (4) neatness and organization. When you first get the examination, look for the weight assigned to each question. This is usually in terms of percentage points. If the value of each question is not given, ask the instructor or test proctor if all questions have equal value. Next, calculate the time you will spend on each question in proportion to its percent of value. Read the directions and each question carefully. It is important that you understand exactly what is asked, and answer that completely. You will not get credit for answering questions that are not on the exam. This is one of the most common errors students make: They write lengthy, well-organized, and eloquent answers to questions they were not asked. Furthermore, you must answer *all parts* of questions. Many questions have two or more parts. Pay special attention to directional words (see Table 8-4).

Think through your answer before you start to write it. If necessary, use additional paper for outlining your answers. The proper sequence is to think first and write second. Two or three minutes of thoughtful planned organizing is worth fifteen or twenty minutes of hurried, disorganized

TABLE 8-4

Essay Test Terms

The following terms may be useful to you in answering test questions of any kind. Learn them—they may save your grade.

Compare: examine the qualities or characteristics in order to discover resemblances. The term implies that you are to emphasize similarities, although differences may be mentioned.

Contrast: stress the dissimilarities, differences, or unlikeness of associated things, events, or problems.

Criticize: express your judgment with respect to the correctness or merit of the factors under consideration; limitations and good points of the plan or work in question.

Define: cite concise, clear, authoritative meanings; details are not required, but boundaries or limitations of the definition should be briefly cited. Keep in mind the class to which a thing belongs and whatever differentiates the particular object from all others in the class.

Describe: recount, characterize, sketch, or relate in narrative form.

Diagram: present a drawing, chart, plan, or relate in narrative form.

Discuss: examine, analyze carefully, and present considerations pro and con regarding the problems or items involved.

Enumerate or List: recount one by one, in concise form, the points required.

Evaluate: present a careful appraisal of the problem, stressing both advantages and limitations.

Explain: clarify, elucidate, and interpret the material you present; state the "how" or "why," reconcile any differences in opinion or experimental results, and, where possible, state causes.

Illustrate: explain or clarify your answer to the problem by presenting a figure, picture, diagram, or concrete example.

Interpret: translate, exemplify, solve or comment upon the subject and give your judgment or reaction to the problem.

Justify: prove or show grounds for decisions; present evidence in a convincing form.

Outline: give the main points and essential supplementary materials, omitting minor details, and present the information in a systematic arrangement or classification.

Prove: establish something with certainty by evaluating and citing experimental evidence or logical reasoning.

Relate: show the relationship or analyze and comment briefly in organized sequence upon the major points of the problem.

Review: analyze and comment briefly in organized sequence upon the major points of the problem.

State: express the high points in brief, clear narrative form.

Summarize: give in condensed form, the main points or facts; secondary details, illustrations, and elaboration are to be omitted.

Trace: give a description of progress, historical sequence, or development from the point of origin.

---

writing. As you survey the complete exam, you will get an idea of what belongs in each question. An outline is the best method of presorting your thoughts. This will assist you in putting the right information in the right question. Start with the question you feel most comfortable answering; this will reduce anxiety and get you off to a faster start. Well-organized answers require planning the major points and writing clear introductions. Your initial sentence should be the best possible one-sentence answer of the entire question. Subsequent sentences should elaborate your first sentence.

It is a good strategy to write for an uninformed reader, not your instructor. Assume that the person who reads your answers will have little or no knowledge of the subject. Your job is to educate him or her. Therefore, you must write legibly, clearly, and completely. Of course, your instructor will read your answers to see how well you inform the mythical uninformed reader. You should reread each answer before moving to the next question. This should be a critical reading in which you correct errors. Common student errors include:

- Omitted words.
- Inappropriate references.
- Errors in grammar.
- Misspelled words.
- Arithmetic errors.
- Inappropriate formulas.
- Improper punctuation.

Whenever possible, provide specific as well as general information—use the technical vocabulary of the course. Include all *relevant* information you can remember. It is better to have too many facts and details than it is to have too few. Also, include examples to clarify your responses.

Essay Test Checklist

Check the boxes in front of all the steps you take when completing an essay test.

☐ 1. Budget your time for each question in proportion to the value of the answers.
☐ 2. Read all the directions carefully and reread portions that are unclear.
☐ 3. Read the entire examination before writing answers to questions.
☐ 4. Be sure you know what is meant by directional words such as *define, compare, discuss,* and *explain.*
☐ 5. Begin with the easiest question first.
☐ 6. Before starting to write the answers, make an outline of major and secondary points.
☐ 7. Underline or star key words or phrases in each question.
☐ 8. If there are relationships between questions, point them out.
☐ 9. If you do not know the answer to a question, try to reason it out.
☐ 10. If you run short of time, outline the remaining questions or present partial answers rather than leave questions unanswered.

☐ 11. Check your paper thoroughly and correct all errors in spelling, punctuation, and grammar before turning it in.

OPEN-BOOK EXAMINATION

Like an essay test, an open-book examination measures your ability to organize data and present ideas. *This is not an easy test.* Too many students minimize the difficulty in writing a good open-book examination. Some open-book examinations are written in class, while others are completed at home. The following tips will help you to write good open-book answers.

1. *Do not waste your time.* Budget your time. Review your notes and get the needed books and articles.

2. *Organize study material into broad topics.* It is important that you can quickly find material pertaining to specific questions.

3. *Outline your answers before you start writing complete responses.* This will allow you to see the gaps in your approach as well as collect additional materials to supplement those you have.

4. *Write concise and to the point answers.* Write your answers in your own words, using quotations and references to support your answers. Do not overuse quotations. Most students tend to use too many quotations. This often results in instructors marking answers down because the students do not adequately demonstrate they understand the material.

5. *If it is possible, type your answers or get someone to type them for you.*

6. *Proofread your answers and correct errors before you give the exam to the instructor.*

AFTER THE EXAMINATION

You can improve your test-taking ability by reviewing returned exams in order to determine what you did wrong. Too many students only look to see their grade and how many questions they answered correctly. Test-taking is a skill you can improve by understanding why you answered questions correctly or incorrectly. Learning a course does not end with taking a test. On the contrary, it ends when you do not repeat your errors. When test questions are reviewed in class, do not argue with the instructor about questions you believe are poorly worded or incorrectly scored. It is better to do this in a private conference. In this way, neither you nor the instructor will be publicly embarrassed. Instructors will seldom adjust test scores if they are verbally attacked in public and none will do so—not even in private—if you cannot prove your case. Approach your instructors in a calm, well-reasoned manner. Getting angry with an instructor and accusing him or her of being unfair is similar to beligerently accusing a coach or a referee of being unfair. You will lose more than a few points; you might also be thrown out of the academic game.

Learn from your mistakes.

Chapter 9

WRITING GOOD PAPERS

Speaking, not writing, is the easiest act for most people. Unless you are a creative artist, writing is hard work. The major difference between the good writer and the poor one is that the good writer approaches writing systematically. Generally, good writers:

- Have a clear focus on the topic.
- Do not begin to write until they have all, or most, facts and information they need.
- Do not use two words when one will do.
- Revise and polish drafts as necessary to produce a smooth final copy.
- Understand that hard writing makes easy reading.

Like good athletes, good writers practice. You cannot learn skillful writing simply by reading books. You must practice writing if you wish to improve your academic game. But practice per se will not get the job done; you must practice the correct ways to convey information. This is a difficult, time-consuming process. It is the process of drafting, editing, and rewriting material.

UNDERSTAND THE ASSIGNMENT

Instructors vary in the manner in which they explain written assignments. Some instructors include explanations in the course syllabus, while others give oral explanations. If you are unclear about the following questions, ask your instructor before you begin writing.

1. *When is the paper due?* Do not be penalized for turning your paper in late. It is your responsibility to have papers ready when they are due. Do not expect an instructor to remind you before papers are due—some will but most will not.

2. *What are acceptable topics for the paper?* Some instructors will allow you to write papers on any topics that interest you as long as they pertain to the course; other instructors assign topics; and many instructors provide a list of acceptable topics. Make certain you know what topics are acceptable.

3. *In what format must the paper be written?* If an instructor prefers or requires a specific format (e.g., specific headings, margins, reference notations), follow it. Do not risk getting a lower grade because your paper does not meet an instructor's format.

4. *What type of information must be included in the paper?* If your paper must include references from journals or magazines or books or a combination of these sources, be sure to have adequate information. Do not provide printed references when the assignment calls for your own subjective analysis or field observations.

5. *How many pages long must the paper be?* Many students lose points because their papers are too long or too short. When an instructor states that a paper should be a specific length (e.g., 10 pages) or within a range (e.g., 10-20 pages), keep your length within the guideline. You are not likely to be penalized if your paper is slightly longer or slightly shorter than required, but you can avoid anxiety about this if you stay within the instructor's guideline. When no length is given, be prudent. A good paper is similar to a good swimming suit: It is long enough to cover the subject and short enough not to be boring.

PREPARE A SCHEDULE

At the beginning of the semester or quarter or whenever you receive an assignment to write a paper, calculate how much time you have before it is due. Based on the difficulty of the assignment, availability of materials, and other course assignments, you should plan to write the paper in five basic stages.

1. Organize your thoughts.
2. Collect information.
3. Write a draft of the paper.
4. Revise and rewrite the draft.
5. Polish the revision; put the paper in final form.

When papers comprise a large proportion of total course points and, therefore, your final grade, it is wise to begin the writing process as soon as possible. Students who cram for tests are also likely to put off until the last few days writing papers. If you have this bad habit, break it!

ORGANIZE YOUR THOUGHTS

The best student papers convey information as clearly as possible. In order to do this, you must think clearly. Good writers think through what they are going to write *before* they put anything on paper. The following pages offer a step-by-step plan that you may find helpful. Whether you use this plan or another one, adhere to a plan only if it helps you.

Clarify Your Purpose

There are three basic reasons for writing a term paper: (1) to direct the reader, (2) to inform the reader, and (3) to persuade the reader. All three reasons are concerned with who, what, when, where, and how of the topics. This means that you must know the general purpose for writing the paper. If you are unclear, ask your instructor. Only when it is clear to you why you are writing a paper will you make it clear to anyone else. "To get a good grade" or "Because the course syllabus requires it" are not adequate purposes.

Define the Limits of Your Subject

Your purpose in writing and the needs of the instructor will place limits on the subject. Above all else, most instructors want you to demonstrate that you understand the topic of your paper. Although it will be read by your instructor, your paper should be written with an uninformed reader in mind.

Write a Statement of Purpose

If you write out an informal statement that identifies your purpose, limits of the subject, and reader, you will have a good foundation upon which to begin creating a paper. This statement should, whenever possible, be a single sentence. An example of such a statement is: "To persuade an uninformed reader that student-athletes benefit academically from competition in sports." Keep your statement with you during the remainder of the writing process. You may revise it, but you should refer to it throughout the various stages of writing.

List Specific Ideas

Now, you are ready to generate ideas about possible titles. A good approach is to brainstorm ideas—list as many ideas as possible. Do not worry about how your ideas sound. After you have exhausted your ideas, go through the list and criticize, eliminate, or combine them. Write the best ideas beneath your statement of purpose.

Plan Your Approach

Begin your research with the information you already have about the subject. Write down major and minor points which you believe are essential to writing a good paper. Draft a *tentative outline* to help you conceptualize the major and minor points. Do not think of the outline as being complete. It is a starting point.

Locate Sources of Information

Each college or university has a major library which is a marvelous source of information. Some of the library resources available to you include:

- *The card catalog.* This is an alphabetical listing of materials in the library with their location or "call" numbers. Materials can be found by looking for them alphabetically under (1) an author's name, (2) the subject, and (3) a publication title.
- *Publications indexes.* Many professions have an index to their journals. Examples of indexes are the *Reader's Guide* and the *Education Index.* Periodical indexes are arranged alphabetically by subjects and authors, with a list of titles of articles and journals, including volume, pages, and date.
- *General references.* Near the information desk are encyclopedia and dictionaries which can help you survey broad subject areas. Some fields of knowledge have their own encyclopedia and dictionaries. Librarians can familiarize you with general references in specific fields.

COLLECT INFORMATION

Most term papers require bibliographies and notes. Perhaps nothing is more distasteful to many students than doing the hard, tedious work of preparing a working bibliography and collecting data for papers. Therefore, they tend to go to the library, grab the first two or three books they find pertaining to the topic, and write a paper. This method is expedient, but it is not the best way to write a paper. In this section we will tell you how to collect information.

Make a Working Bibliography

The purpose of surveying library resources is to locate materials that will help you with your subject. First, you should prepare a *working bibliography* which lists the references you might use in your research. Your final bibliography will consist of only the references you actually used. You can compile your working bibliography on loose sheets of paper, but it is better to prepare it on index cards. Index cards are easier to handle, edit, and arrange for use (see Figure 10). You probably will collect more references than you use. Your cards can be compiled as follows:

- In the upper left hand corner of each card, list the author's name. Underneath the author's name, write the title of the publication, the edition, the place of publication, the publisher, and the date. If no date is given, write "n.d." (no date). If a book is a translation, include the name of the translator and write "trans." after his or her name. If a book is edited, write "ed." (editor) after the author's name.
- In the upper right hand corner, number the card. Use this number on all subsequent cards that contain information from this source.
- In the lower left hand corner, write the library call number so that you will not have to look it up every time you use the book.
- Group your cards by subject matter under the topics that correspond with the major points in your tentative outline.

When you have completed your working bibliography, you are ready to collect the information you need.

Evaluate the Information

A good writer knows how to handle references. As you develop your writing skills, you will learn to recognize the value of a reference by its author, date of publication, and soundness of content. This is nothing more than becoming a reference critic. If you have learned to be critical of other persons' athletic abilities, you can learn to be critical of the academic abilities of writers—even if you never become an outstanding scholar yourself.

Learn to Skim

In order to optimally use your time, learn how to skim a book or article to decide whether it may be useful for you. If you believe it is, survey it to be certain. Look over the table of contents, headings, and index. Skim paragraphs and other portions of the book before deciding to read it from cover to cover.

Make Complete and Accurate Notes

After you read a reference and decide it is useful, start making notes. It is imperative that your notes are accurate and written in a manner that you can understand later (see Figure 11). Unless you record accurate notes, your term paper will be gravely flawed. The following tips will help you make useful notes.

- *Write in ink.* Pencil notes wear off from continuous handling.
- *Keep each idea on a separate card, and write the subject in the upper left corner.* This will enable you to have all of the cards on the same subject together.

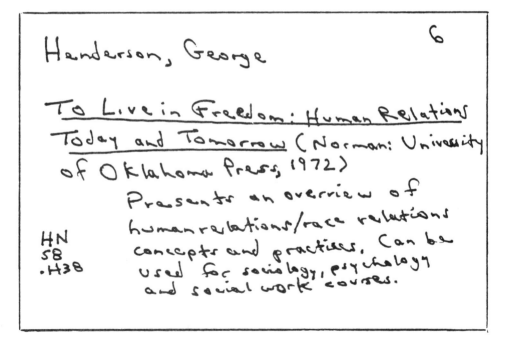

Figure 10. Bibliography card.

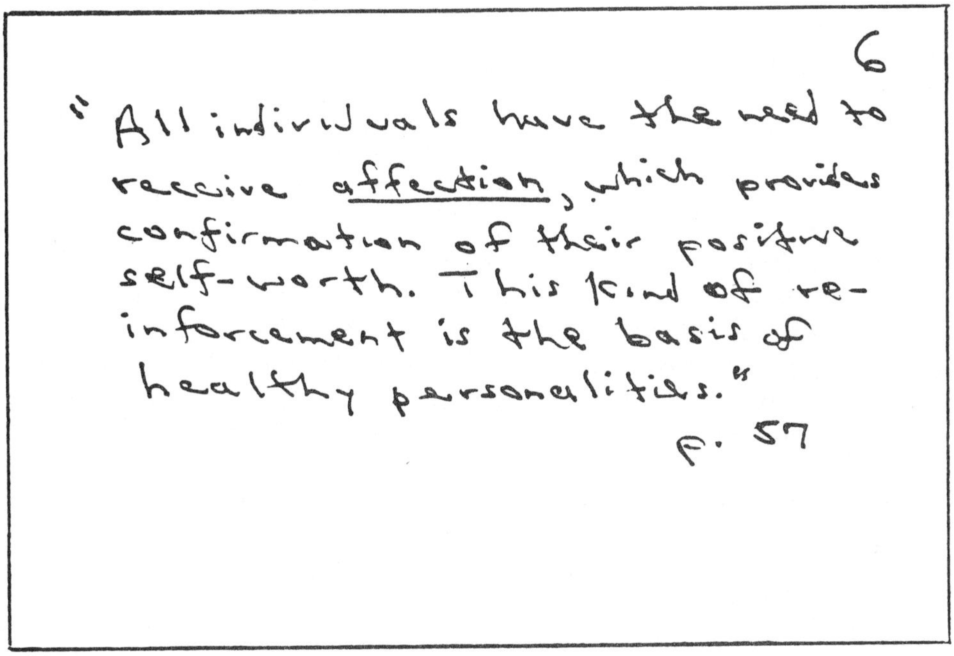

Figure 11. Note card.

- *In the upper right corner write the source number.*
- *At the end of a quotation or statement, write the page or pages where you found it.*

Use discretion. Most students make too many notes. If you wish to copy most of a book, do not make notes. It is quicker and easier to make a photographic copy. But this will only result in collecting a lot of unneeded material. Again, be discreet.

Put it in your own words. You are likely to understand the material better if you make notes in your own words. In addition, you are apt to exercise better judgment when writing ideas in your own words. Use as few direct quotes as possible, but credit other persons when you paraphrase. Do not plagiarize.

Interpret fairly. You must interpret each author fairly. This means that you will not read your own ideas into what the author says. Use separate note cards for your own ideas, or put brackets or a circle around them.

Keep an open mind. As you read the materials, stay objective and keep an open mind. Do not try to prove preconceived notions by using only data that support your views and discard data that do not. In short, be ready to change your mind if the facts warrant it.

COMPLETE YOUR RESEARCH

Do not ask your friends or your instructor to tell you when to conclude your research. You must decide when to wrap it up. This is a judgment call, and it requires good judgment. Whenever possible, start to think about ending your research when you have substantial knowledge of the subject. And end your research when you know as much about your topic as you need to know. In other words, get all the facts and information you need before completing the research.

It is impossible to write a good report or paper without an adequate knowledge of the subject. None of the tips in this book are worth much if you have not done enough research. Sometimes students say: "The paper seemed to write itself." Of course, papers do not write themselves; but if you know enough about a topic, the writing comes more quickly than when you know very little.

Survey your research. Find out how much information you have collected and what is missing. You may have lots of data but most of it focuses on only a few of your major points. You need to have an idea of what and how much more information you still need.

Examine your findings critically. Once you have collected what seems to be adequate information, evaluate your evidence. Ask yourself, "Do I have enough to write a convincing paper?" Put your findings in the most orderly form possible, and then evaluate what you have. The sheer volume of your notes should not be the major criterion of adequacy. Look for quality.

Formulate a tentative conclusion. Your tentative conclusion must be a logical result of your data, e.g., "Students benefit academically from athletic competition if they are adequately prepared to compete." Check your conclusion to see if your evidence supports it. If it does, you are ready to organize your material for writing the paper. If it does not, you must find additional material or rethink your conclusion.

ORGANIZE YOUR MATERIAL

The most important phase of the writing process is organizing your material. Most students who get low grades have enough material to get high grades, but their papers are disorganized. Instructors frequently read only a few paragraphs of poorly organized papers. If you do not put your material in a logical sequence, you will not be able to present your best case. It is sad when students get poor grades because of their failure to correctly organize adequate material which they have worked hard to get.

Let your form follow the material. Course material dictates its own pattern. Your job is to select a format that best fits your material. Then organize the material in the most logical and effective order.

Use a sound framework. Most reports follow a basic framework: (1) introduction, (2) body, and (3) conclusion. The introduction must capture the reader's attention, establish rapport, and state your purpose. The body must be a compilation of ideas. And the conclusion must summarize the main points presented in the body and it must also bring the paper to a smooth end.

Organize the Body of Your Material

The hardest part of writing a paper is arranging the material for the body into an effective sequence. It is best to organize the body of your material in the following stages:

Stage 1

Use your statement of purpose. Reread your statement of purpose and decide whether the material you have collected is relevant or irrelevant. This is another check in the process.

Stage 2

Determine the points you want to make. Omit words, ideas, and facts that are not essential to the understanding or acceptance of your objective. If you have done your research well, you are likely to have too much material rather than too little. Collecting words for a paper is like collecting toys—it is difficult to get rid of them, even useless words. As painful and ego-deflating as it may be, you must define, sift, and discard material until only essential material is left.

Stage 3

Identify your main ideas. Distinguish between main and subordinate ideas. Main ideas are so important that leaving one out unbalances the rest. You must also distinguish main ideas from the facts, figures, or examples that support them. For example, the main ideas in describing a car are the body, chassis, engine, and transmission; while the subordinate ideas are parts such as windows, seats, fan belt, and pistons. Or stated another way, the main ideas about a car are performance, economy, and reliability; while items such as 55 miles an hour, 25 miles per gallon, and few repairs are supporting ideas.

Stage 4

Choose an effective organization pattern. You must arrange your main ideas into an order that leads your reader logically to your conclusion. This means that you must select the pattern or combination of patterns that will most effectively reach your reader. Below are the keys to well organized papers.

- Select the pattern that will *best communicate your ideas.* You must know how you wish to present your material.
- As a rule, follow the scientific method of *inductive reasoning:* general conclusions flow logically out of specific observations. Of course, you can use the deductive method (set up a general premise and then prove it), but the inductive method is more emphatic. The inductive paper is like a good mystery novel; the author and the reader arrive at the conclusion at the same time.
- Lead your reader *from the familiar to the new.* Start with something the reader understands and gradually give him or her new ideas, either proving or disproving familiar ideas.
- Go from the *simple to the complex.* When attempting to explain a difficult subject, start with the simplest part. Good papers do not jump from the simple to the complex—there are varying degrees of complex parts in between them. Nor do they move from the complex to the simple.
- Arrange your points to give *maximum emphasis.* Like a good mystery, build your argument to a logical climax. Because the final position is the most important, this is where you should put your best material. Like athletic competition, you should put forth your best performance in the finals, not the preliminaries. If you make your best points before the end of your report, the ending becomes anticlimactic.

Stage 5

Outline your material. A student who begins to write a paper without an outline is similar to an athlete who prepares to run a marathon without a training schedule. She may be able to finish the race, but she would do much better if she had sketched out a training routine and followed it. Writing a top quality paper is not the same as writing a short letter or a brief impromptu report. An outline provides a checklist of things you want to include, and helps you to place items in the most effective order.

Outlining is much easier than most students believe. Once you have collected your material and organized it according to a pattern, you can use an outline to fill in the facts and ideas. Save the introduction and conclusion until later. Below is an example of a working outline.

(*Introduction*)
1. First main idea.
   a. Fact and reasoning to support this idea.
      (1) Fact and reasoning to support a.
      (2) Additional fact and reasoning to support a.

       (a) Support for (2).

       (b) Additional support for (2).

   b. Additional fact and reasoning to support 1.

     (1) Support for b.

     (2) Additional support for b.

 2. Second main idea.

   a. Fact and reasoning to support this idea.

   b. Etc.

(*Conclusion*)

The more complex your outline, the easier it will be for you to write the paper later. But remember that an outline does not have to be all inclusive. If you try to put every detail into an outline, you will waste time and effort that can be devoted to writing the paper. Some outlines are merely main ideas on a piece of paper, while others are notes on cards arranged in a logical order.

Final Steps

Once you have a suitable outline, the final steps are: (1) to plan for transitions to bring together your main and supporting ideas, (2) to plan your introduction, and (3) to plan your conclusion.

Plan for transitions. Transitions link successive ideas and they relate individual ideas to the overall purpose of the paper. Linking successive ideas is called the *minor transition.* This is done by the use of words or phrases such as "then" and "but of least importance." Minor transitions alert the reader that he or she is moving to new elements.

The second linking function—relating individual ideas to the overall purpose—is called the *major transition.* This transition may also be used to summarize the paper to that moment and anticipate the next development of ideas. It is often helpful to tell the reader how seemingly unrelated concepts are interrelated. Both minor and major transitions help you to keep your arguments and data relevant.

Plan for an introduction. Your introduction should capture the readers' interest, focus their attention on the subject, and ease them into the subject. Therefore, you must decide carefully what points you want to include in your introduction.

Plan the conclusion. An effective conclusion summarizes the paper's content.

WRITING A FIRST DRAFT

It may sound silly but the best way to start writing a paper is to start. You should not worry about writing a perfect first draft; get your ideas on paper as quickly as possible. Later, you can edit, rewrite, and smooth out what you have written. The following ideas will help you write a first draft.

Double-space everything. It is easier to read what you have written if you double space it, even indented quotations that will be single-spaced in the final draft. Quadruple-space between paragraphs and leave generous margins. Contrary to popular opinion, this is not a waste of paper. You will be able to move quickly and carefully read, edit, and change the paper if it is written this way. This is true whether you type your paper or write it in longhand.

Do not worry about the introduction. Most students spend their time foolishly trying to write the "perfect" introduction. They take days to begin writing as they wait for inspiration. It would be nice to write such an introduction, but it is seldom done, and it is almost never done in the first draft. Do not worry about the introduction; start with the main body of the report. Or, if you must write something, polish it later. Do not wait for inspiration. It may never come.

Do not get bogged down by your outline. Outlines should serve you, not enslave you. A good working outline is more a sketch to be filled in or altered than a blueprint to be rigidly followed. Do not let your outline slow you down. If you find that it is slowing you down, put it aside or revise it.

Finish one part at a time. Break your paper into manageable parts or sections and concentrate on only one part at a time. If you try to simultaneously write bits and pieces of the whole paper, you are likely to bog down and finish none of the parts—or finish all of them inadequately.

Write as much as possible each time. Good writers discipline themselves to write as much as they can at each sitting. Do not worry about how the material fits together, put it down as it comes to you. If you must pause, try to finish whatever you are working on. When you are ready to start writing again, reread what you have written.

Do not revise as you write. Once you start writing, you will be anxious to finish the paper, but wait until you complete the first draft before you edit, rewrite, and polish it. The reason for this is that trying to revise at the same time you write the first draft interrupts the flow of ideas. This delay in revisions pertains to spelling and grammar, too. You can attend to these things after you finish the first draft.

Concentrate on content. As you write your first draft, try to make it as complete as possible. It is better to have too much detail at this stage than too little. A general rule of thumb is that it is easier to take things out when you polish your paper than to try to fill in topics and details. Remember that simple subject-verb-object sentences are best, but complex sentences add variety.

Explain and illustrate. An instructor is not likely to be satisfied with your papers if they lack substance. You will probably get your papers back with marginal comments asking for specific examples that illustrate the points you have tried to make. Papers that have illustrations and explanations help the reader to understand the topic.

Know when to stop. Finishing the first draft is like feeding the reader a meal. You should stop when he or she has enough. This is usually when you have included all the material you need to make your major and minor points. You may be tempted to add more material but this will result in a rambling paper—you will stuff the reader. Make your beginnings and endings best. Your first and last words are the most important in paragraphs.

GUIDE TO EDITING, REWRITING, AND POLISHING YOUR PAPER

When you review and edit your paper, shift your viewpoint to the reader's. Wait a day or two before editing, then read the paper three times, focusing on particular issues each time. Some people edit better when they read aloud. When you find something that sounds awkward, confusing, or long-winded, revise it.

First Reading

During your first reading, check the *content:*

- Does it contain enough information?
- Has too much material been included?
- Do the facts need more interpretation?
- Are the sources the best available to you?
- Is the writing based on sound reasoning?

Second Reading

During your second reading, check the *organization:*

- Is the subject stated clearly?
- Is the subject divided into clear-cut stages?
- Is the connection between stages clear?

Third Reading

During your third reading, check *sentence structure, diction,* and *typographical style:*

- Are sentences correct?
- Are words specific and concrete?
- Is the typographical style consistent?
- Can you improve sentences by varying sentence length?

General Review

Ask a friend to review your paper. This will serve as a check against your own review. Ask your friend to answer honestly the following questions:

- *Purpose:* Is the purpose stated clearly? If so, is the clarity attained through a logical development of the subject?
- *Assumptions:* If assumptions are stated, do they appear to be reasonable?
- *Objectivity:* Are all issues explored with reasonable impartiality? Is there an objective appraisal of alternatives, and does it result in the best choice or final position?
- *Credibility:* Are the arguments supported by facts? Are the facts interpreted logically? Are the conclusions drawn from arguments presented in the paper?
- *Conclusions:* Do conclusions flow logically from the body of the paper?
- *Style:* Is the paper written well and grammatically correct?

If friends critique your paper, do not become defensive. Thank them; they are doing you a favor. Do not argue with them if their opinion differs from your own. It is your job to convince a reader to like what you have written. This is done by putting your best thoughts in the paper. Use your own review and, when available, your friends' review to edit, rewrite, and polish papers (see Figure 12).

Final Checklist

Check the boxes in front of the statements that apply to you.

Main Goal
□ 1. I try to communicate clearly and effectively in each paper.

Content
□ 1. The content I select is really worth communicating to my reader.
□ 2. I do my best to make each paper interesting for my reader.
□ 3. I use only content which is related to my thesis statement.
□ 4. I use facts and good logic to support my generalizations.
□ 5. I use specific details to communicate exactly what is in my mind.

Organization
□ 1. Each paper has a thesis that states the main idea I wish to communicate.
□ 2. Each paper has an introduction, a middle and a conclusion.
□ 3. Each paper has several clear main points to support my thesis.
□ 4. These points are arranged so that the most important one comes *last*.
□ 5. Each of my paragraphs is organized around a good topic sentence.

forerunner of modern rehabilitation centers. Although the
center's initial efforts centered on helping children with disabilities,
it later expanded to include adults. ~~with disabilities~~

Other private organizations ~~that are~~ (well-known) ~~to us~~
~~today~~ began during this period. The Salvation Army, ~~one of the~~ *for example,*
~~nation's best known organizations,~~ began in England in 1878
and expanded to the United States in 1880. The Goodwill
Industries was organized in ~~America~~ *this country* (in 1902) by Edgar J. Helms,
a Methodist minister. *Primarily individual religious groups initiated* ~~The~~ major efforts to get persons with disabilities
into the mainstream of society ~~were made primarily by private~~
~~individuals and religion-affiliated groups.~~ The first totally
American, state-supported institution designed to aid the poor
was established in 1897, the Minnesota State Hospital for
Indigent and Dependent Children. ~~As the name implies, it was~~
Although it was set up not (exclusively) for patients with disabilities, *this hospital treated* ~~however,~~ a substantial
number of them ~~were treated there~~ because ~~of their~~
~~inability to afford~~ private care *was unaffordable*

<u>Biblical and Other Literature</u>

Many ~~of the~~ ancient myths and stereotypes of people with disabilities [s]
~~are~~ still ~~believed today,~~ *exist.* ~~while~~ *Although* few persons currently sub-
scribe to abandoning or killing people with disabilities, many ~~persons~~ *do*
associate disabilities with sin and the Devil. ~~When most~~
~~people think about or see persons with disabilities,~~ they
either consciously or subconsciously think that disability is
the synonym of bad. More often than not, "able-bodied" is
associated with good, *i.e.,* ~~e.g., with~~ Christ and the angels, ~~with~~

Figure 12. Revised draft of a research paper.

Correctness
- ☐ 1. I check for errors in grammar and punctuation, especially those which might confuse the reader.
- ☐ 2. I write complete sentences and do not run any sentences together.
- ☐ 3. I check my spelling.
- ☐ 4. I check references and footnotes or endnotes for accuracy.
- ☐ 5. I type my papers or have them typed and then I proof read them carefully.

Style

☐ 1. I check for awkward and unclear wording which might not communicate my thoughts.

☐ 2. I use a dictionary to check any doubtful word selection.

☐ 3. My sentences are varied so that they will not be monotonous to read.

☐ 4. I write long sentences only if I am sure I can control them.

☐ 5. I try to express my ideas honestly and directly.

Chapter 10

PROFILES OF EXCELLENCE
AND COURAGE

A "jock" is an athlete who consciously tries to push aside human qualities such as intelligence, compassion, and social awareness. He or she defines life as a game to be won at any cost and by whatever means are necessary. Socially and academically, jocks are several years behind their peers. In their most crass condition, slovenly dressed jocks can be observed loudly burping, sniffling, and yawning in public places. They are Neanderthal people in the twentieth century. This is the image most athletes loathe. And this is the image you must be careful not to project.

It is difficult for the general public to accept as representatives of athletes, male and female scholars who are able to give an interview without stringing together a series of "uh," "you know," and "er." It is equally difficult for the general public to imagine superstars as being concerned with someone or something outside their own skins. Yet, the truly great athletes are better known for their respect for others and goals beyond winning medals.

In addition, given the disproportionate representation of black men and women in sports, particularly those known in collegiate circles as "revenue-producing" sports, it seems important to point out, as Dr. Harry Edwards, the well-known black sociologist says

> ...there are still just over 1,400 black people (up from 1,100 before the establishment of the United States Football League) making a living as professional athletes in the three major sports today. And if one added to this number all the black athletes making a living in all other American sports, all the blacks making a living in minor and semiprofessional sports leagues, and all the black trainers, coaches, and doctors making a living in professional sports, there would still be less than 2,400 black Americans making a living in professional athletics today.

The authors believe that while Dr. Edwards makes his point specifically to black athletes, it is important for all student-athletes to bear in mind that last year's all stater, like yesterday's newspaper, is of little interest to anyone.

135

There is nothing sadder than to speak with an adult who focuses on "what might have been" instead of what is. It is your responsibility to approach your academic activities with the same degree of dedication and expectation of success as you approach your athletic activities. Do not be sold on the idea that your athletic abilities will take care of you, they won't, except in extremely rare cases. Again, quoting from Dr. Edwards:

> ... it must be made unequivocally clear that in the last analysis, it is black student athletes themselves who must shoulder a substantial portion of the responsibility for improving their own circumstances. Education is an activist pursuit and cannot in reality be "given." It must be obtained "the old fashion way"—one must earn it! Black student athletes, therefore, must insist upon educational discipline no less than athletic discipline among themselves, and they must insist upon educational integrity in athletic programs rather than, as is all too often the case, merely seeking the most parsimonious academic route to maintaining athletic eligibility. The bottom line here is that if black student athletes fail to take an active role in establishing and legitimizing a priority upon academic achievement, nothing done by any other party to this American sports tragedy will matter—if for no other reason than the fact that a slave cannot be freed against his will.

To illustrate the qualities which are the direct opposite of the "jock," the qualities which we believe can and should be embodied in most student-athletes, we have selected two articles to be reprinted about two outstanding scholar-athletes: Stefan Humphries and Peggy Neppel Darrah.

Stefan and Peggy, one male and one female, one black and one white, one ending in joy and the other ending in sorrow, are people whose athletic accomplishments are beyond the grasp of most competitors. However, what is important about their stories is that their lives reflect the highest achievements of character and integrity in quite different ways, and, above all, Stefan and Peggy remind us that there is much more to life than excelling in sports.

HE CAME OUT PICTURE PERFECT

Douglas S. Looney

It was a rollicking affair at the University of Michigan graduation ceremony the other day in Ann Arbor. Gathered in the football stadium, perhaps 4,300 of the school's 5,700 graduates-to-be—the other 1,400 apparently having business appointments—were determined to party. Champagne corks popped like rifle shots and then arched into the perfect blue sky. Some of the revelers wore Mickey Mouse ears, others propellers on their mortar-boards. One sported a Baltimore Oriole baseball cap.

When university president Harold Shapiro told the good-timing throng, "This is the first and probably last time you'll sit on the 50-yard line," everyone booed. And when Walter Cronkite, who gave the commencement address, said he understood that venturing out into the world might create a feeling for the new grads "bordering on panic," they laughed. Mostly, though, they popped champagne corks and acted crazy. Looking terribly ill at ease amid the chaos was one Stefan Humphries, a varsity football player and an engineering major, with an interdisplinary concentration in biology. Once he self-consciously took a sip (a very small sip) of champagne. Once he raised an arm tentatively in celebration. Mostly he looked as if he wished he were elsewhere. "Graduation is supposed to be somber and conservative," Humphries said later. "I don't think you yell until you leave. I never yell about anything until it's all over with."

Yet if any of these students had a reason to go bonkers, it was Humphries. "He is the true image of the scholar-athlete," says James J. Duderstadt, dean of the College of Engineering. Indeed, in an age when too many football players never get it straight that attending class is thought by some to be a part of the college experience, Humphries is a beacon. Four years ago, we celebrated him as the ideal mix of great student, great athlete, and great person from a great family (*SI*, May 26, 1980, *The Can't Miss Kid*) as he emerged from St. Thomas Aquinas High in Fort Lauderdale. That appraisal was, if anything, not extravagant enough. Says Michigan athletic director Don Canham, "He's such a remarkable kid. He's lived up to and beyond his billing."

All Humphries did at Michigan, one of the premier universities—public or private—in the nation, was march through a course schedule that appears to have been designed by a sadist. It included such guts as engineering thermodynamics and electrobiophysics. With a 3.67 gradepoint, he was named Outstanding Student in the engineering school "very humbling," says Humphries. "I've encountered some very bright people."

In one remarkable streak of academic prowess, stretching from the spring of 1981 through the summer of 1982, he took 15 courses for 45 hours of credit. Result: eight A pluses, six A's, one B plus. Indeed, during one blitz, Humphries received nothing but A's and A pluses for three semesters. Finally, when he stumbled to a B in network analysis, a course having nothing whatsoever to do with ABC or CBS, football coach Bo Schembechler called Humphries in and said, "Congratulations on being human." Humphries didn't smile.

Another time, Schembechler summoned Humphries and said, "Aren't you doing too much studying?"

"No," said Humphries.

"Are you enjoying Michigan?"

"Yes."

"And you're getting out some?"

"Yes."

"Are you sure you're enjoying yourself?"

"I'm enjoying myself, Bo, but I've got to go study."

As gorgeous as Humphries' transcript is, it doesn't reflect his true academic excellence. At Michigan, an A plus is worth no more in GPA computation than an A, and Humphries earned nine A pluses to go with his 15 A's. "I didn't come to Michigan to get all A's," he says. "I came to learn." And, as you might suspect by now, he did it all in four years, a feat Duderstadt calls "very rare." Most Michigan engineering students take 4½ to five years to earn their degrees.

Humphries belongs to all kinds of honorary societies, including Tau Beta Pi, the engineering equivalent of Phi Beta Kappa, and ranks among the top 10 percent of the 1,081 graduating seniors in the engineering school. "He's as big mentally and humanly as he is physically," says Lee Quackenbush, assistant dean of the engineering school, and Humphries is 6'4", 262 pounds. The only documented dumb thing he ever did at Michigan occurred when he arrived as a freshman and was asked to fill out a form listing his "non-athletic activities, hobbies, interests." Wrote Humphries, "Swimming, tennis." In January, *The Detroit News* named him one of its 10 Michiganians of the Year, a list that included Lee Iacocca.

On the field, Humphries was, well, just as good. A three-year starter at offensive guard, he was an academic All-American twice, All-Big Ten twice and, last fall, AP first team All-American and a National Football Foundation and Hall of Fame Scholar. His play was brilliant, slipping only occasionally to merely terrific. Schembechler once said that Humphries was the only player on the squad who never had a bad game. Actually, against Illinois last year, Humphries faltered—by his own standards—when he had the angle of his blocks wrong, but that was a mere blip.

Interior, offensive-line coach Paul Schudel says that in grading most players it's simply a matter of asking, "Did he make the block or not?" With Humphries, however, the criteria were more stringent because he would make the block. "In his case, he might block a guy downfield for two or three yards," says Schudel, "but I'll decide that wasn't good enough—for Stefan." Last season, Humphries' average blocking grade was 76. In the Wolverine system 70 is considered good and 75 excellent. During one stretch, Humphries graded out at 91, 82, 81, 81 and 79.

Over the years Michigan has had a host of superior offensive linemen, including Don Dierdorf, Reggie McKenzie, John Geisler, Bubba Paris, Ed Muransky, Dave Gallagher, Mark Donahue, Walt Downing and George Lilja. None was better than Humphries. No wonder Schembechler pushes back in his chair, props his feet on his desk, puffs jauntily on an awful-smelling cigar and chortles, "He's just a beautiful kid."

A beautiful kid heading for medical school—either Michigan or Northwestern in the NFL off-season—who says he might specialize in pediatrics or orthopedics. If he chooses the latter, he may use his engineering background to design artificial limbs. Says Humphries, "I like to work with somebody who can talk to me and tell me if I'm helping." First, though, he'll help the Chicago Bears, who drafted him in the third round. Knocking around his Ann Arbor apartment on draft day in a green scrub outfit, he was asked just after hearing from the Bears on the phone, "Are you satisfied with this?"

"You know I'd never be satisfied with being third in anything," said Humphries, "but it gives me that much more to work for." As a third-round selection, he can expect to receive something like $375,000.00 spread over three years. But Humphries doesn't brood over such things. As Duderstadt says, "He never loses sight of the fact that his primary objective is a medical career. He knows that his scholarly ability will stay with him." As opposed to his lateral speed, which, too soon, will desert him.

Bill Tobin, the Bears' director of player personnel says, "First, we like his intelligence. Second, we like his stability and ability." What Tobin doesn't say is, third, never mind that the NFL in its wisdom selected 70 players ahead of Humphries, he'll be an All-Pro. You can bet the house and spouse on that one.

When all's said and done, though, Humphries' most significant accomplishment may be the glorious example he set as a scholar-athlete. Says Schembechler, "All Stefan Humphries stands for is everything this game is supposed to be about. Football is always important to him, but never, never to the exclusion of academics." And there's the rub. Why can so few athletes successfully combine big-time sports and big-time academics?

Says Anne Monterio, director of academic services for the College of Engineering, "Are athletics and academics incompatible? Well, athletics and engineering—very definitely. Neither side is very giving about relaxing its demands." Canham says, "They're not incompatible, but they're very difficult to combine." Adds Duderstadt, "Usually, you have to compromise on one or the other." Humphries is cautious on the subject of games and brains. Do they mix? Long pause. Real long pause. Finally he says, "They can."

But do they.

Pause. Long pause. Real long pause. At last he says, "It takes a lot of commitment, a lot of discipline. Sometimes I miss out on what the normal student might experience—like getting involved in clubs, time to sit around and talk, go to parties. I used to think how nice it would be to have time to spend an afternoon in a pickup basketball game. I find myself always wanting another hour. Just one more. It's hard to sit up and study when you're tired and your body is sore. It takes inner motivation."

So the two mix, sort of?

Pause. Long pause. Real long pause. Finally he says, "Professors here aren't too tolerant of athletes flunking classes and just getting by. The truth is, playing football at this level is a real disadvantage academically. I have to admit it. But in the growing it makes you do as a person, it's an advantage."

So you could have gotten a better education without football?

Serious silence. Hello? Stefan? The lights are on in there, but is anybody home? Finally, he says quietly, "No." Feel free to translate that as "Yes."

Richard Scott, an engineering professor and Humphries' adviser, agrees. "What's his average—3.6, 3.7?" says Scott. "He's about reaching academic saturation." But obviously racing through Humphries' fertile mind—don't be tricked by his sleepy eyes and his demeanor, which suggest he's stuck for an answer when somebody says hello—are memories of those weeks when football required 50 hours, studying another 30, and classes and labs 15.

Humphries' father, Thornton, is the principal of the Everglades Traditional Middle School in Fort Lauderdale. Thornton makes sure not only that his school gives out the same number of awards for academic achievements as for athletic accomplishments but also that the trophies are the same size. "The two can mix," he says, "but a young person has to want them to mix. The big problem is that sports bring immediate recognition while nobody sees an A being made in chemistry. The benefit of that A is down the road. What has to be emphasized is that education is the way you become successful. Stefan had the background when he went to Michigan to compete academically as well as athletically. However, you don't start preparing for that in high school. You start on the first day of kindergarten."

Pat Haden, a Rhodes scholar who played quarterback on USC's national championship teams in 1972 (consensus) and '74 (UPI) before playing pro ball, says, "Athletics and academics should mix. Why not? It's simply a matter of organizing one's time. Players say they're too busy with football that they don't have time to study. That's not true."

The problem is that a lot of colleges have lost their way in attempting to sort out the academic-athletic conflict. Increasingly they talk of their academics, while continuing to accept young men whose intellectual curiosity extends no further than knowing their time in the 40—on grass and artificial turf. Says Humphries, "I do wish universities would try to improve their academics, putting more emphasis on them and less on football. An athlete should come to school with some priorities in mind. He should make education the first priority. Then he should have alternate career goals outside of sport. Then he should enjoy the college experience. Conversely, if you figure you'll do everything in football and not worry about education, it will not be a positive experience. In college football, anytime you see a guy flunk out, it's a stigma."

Coaches exacerbate the problem. While they publicly stand foursquare behind the idea that their players should excel in the classroom, in truth they have their fingers crossed behind their backs. That's because coaches must win or be fired. Thus, how much can they really be expected to worry about a tight end's progress in European history?

Despite his sometimes outrageous behavior on the sidelines, Schembechler sympathizes with the athletic-academic dilemma as much as any big-time coach. Over the last four years it was virtually impossible to visit with him for more than several minutes before he started riffling through the papers on his desk, looking for a copy of Humphries' record to display. Once he peered down at it, shook his head and said, "I can't even pronounce the names of the classes he's taking." Then there's the time Humphries had to miss practice because of a lab. He walked up to Schembechler and said, "Bo, you're not going to like what I have to tell you, but there's nothing we can do about it." Schembechler tells that story on himself and gets great joy out of it.

Says Mike Wilson, a graduating defensive tackle and Humphries' roommate at Michigan, "School can take away from your concentration on the football field. To try to combine the two is a heckuva problem." George Hoey, Michigan's academic counselor for the jocks, says, "I don't know if athletics and academics are compatible, but Stefan has made them so. It also seems as if he has sailed through. He does it the perfect way, with long-range planning and short-term goals. What sets him apart is that there are a lot of guys with a vast amount of ability on the field who do O.K. in the classroom. What Stefan is saying to them is that O.K. isn't nearly good enough."

How often does a guy like Humphries come along?

"Never. It just doesn't happen," says Hoey.

Humphries is so special his mind has been celebrated at Michigan as much as his body. In one team meeting Schembechler used the word legitimize and then stopped. "Now, Stefan, is legitimize a proven word?" asked Bo. Yes, advised Humphries. Once, while adding numbers on the board, Schembechler turned to Humphries and said, "Is that right, Stefan?" No, advised Humphries.

Yet, in the world of football, brains can be a minus. "I've heard the fact that I want to go to medical school is a detrimental force with the pros," says Humphries. It is. The Bears, for example, checked carefully to make sure football was in Humphries' future. "He told us he wanted to play," says Tobin. "But with these guys with real, real high IQs, there's always a little concern about whether they will."

Go back to draft day. The Seattle Seahawks had sent scout Ralph Goldston to hover over Humphries because they thought they might pick him in the second round, and they wanted to make sure those bad guys from the USFL didn't show up with money hanging out of their pockets. Goldston engaged Humphries in conversation: "You want to be a lawyer or doctor or something?"

"Yes, a doctor."

"Oh, so do you know which medical school you're going to?"

"Not for sure."

"Yeah, well, a medical school is a medical school, right? It don't make no difference, right?"

"It does to me."

"Oh, yeah? Well, I don't know nothing about this medical school crap. So why did you come to Michigan to school?"

"I wanted to build snowmen."

See, what does fluid mechanics have to do with executing a horn block? Different worlds.

Oh yes, did we mention the Rhodes scholarship? As it turns out, Humphries narrowly missed being selected. (About his only other failure in life was when he lost a Florida state spelling bee as a fourth grader by flubbing "outmaneuver"; he reversed the e and u.) Had he received the Rhodes, he would have had to choose between two years at Oxford and pro football. No problem for Humphries. He would have taken the fellowship.

Recently, after dinner at an Ann Arbor Chinese restaurant, Humphries read his fortune from a cookie: "Serious trouble will bypass you." He pondered it, smiled and said, "That's good news." Which is exactly what Stefan Humphries is. But he's not yelling because, remember, he doesn't yell about anything until it's over. And for Humphries, it has only just begun.

STAR ATHLETE LEAVES LEGACY OF COURAGE WITHOUT TEARS

Claudia Waterloo

There were no tears at the memorial service for Peggy Neppel Darrah.

The grieving had been done earlier, during her seven-month battle with cancer. During those last months, after she lost the use of her legs, her indomitable spirit seemed trapped inside a dying body. Her death came as a relief to those who loved her, for it meant she was free from pain.

Peggy Neppel Darrah, who died last month at age 28, was possibly the greatest woman athlete ever at Iowa State University.

Before her legs ultimately failed her, they carried her to three world records for women's long-distance running. Then, at the peak of her athletic career, she gave up competition to pursue a doctorate in animal science at ISU. She was very close to finishing when she died.

No one wept at her memorial service because that's how she would have wanted it. She didn't want people saddened by her illness. With characteristic good humor, she posted a hand-drawn smiley face on her hospital room door. Afraid people would feel awkward visiting her, she passed out coloring books from her hospital bed.

Throughout her illness she maintained the same strategy that won her so many races. "She believed she'd win before the starting gun went off," said her husband, Mark Darrah.

She told a social worker at Mary Greeley Memorial Hospital: "You know, I never lose a race easily."

Peggy Neppel, the second of six children of Alice and Paul Neppel of rural Dolliver, was not particularly agile or coordinated as a child, her mother remembered.

But she wanted to be the best runner in the world, said Chris Murray, the coach at ISU who first recognized her talent and worked with her. "She certainly had the determination. She felt she wanted to develop herself to the maximum."

Murray, now women's track and field coach at the University of Arizona, called his work with Neppel's raw talent "a grand experiment. I see now where I could have gotten Peg to a much higher level...but at the time, these things were just not being done with the female athlete."

Women's varsity sports did not exist at ISU when Neppel enrolled as a freshman prenursing student in 1971. Women's teams were organized on a club basis, and coaches were volunteers.

"When Peg ran, they still wore baggy warmups and piled into station wagons" to attend meets, said Chris Plonsky, women's sports information director at ISU.

Won Championships

Neppel trained by running 100 miles some weeks, a regimen unheard of for women athletes at that time. "Basically, women's cross-country as a collegiate sport was born at Iowa State during that early era," Murray said.

The first official collegiate championships weren't held until Neppel's senior year, when she won the individual title. Iowa State won that first team championship and the next three as well, a feat unmatched in Association of Intercollegiate Athletics for Women competition.

Neppel took five years to complete her undergraduate study, having switched to animal science from prenursing after her sophomore year.

She met Mark Darrah in a cardiovascular physiology class shortly after he came to Iowa State to work on a doctorate in biomedical engineering. They were lab partners, and got to know each other working out together in the gymnasium. Unaware of Neppel's athletic prowess, Darrah started betting her she couldn't beat certain times at running meets.

"I didn't realize how good she was until she started winning all those dinners and banana splits off me," he laughed.

By that time Neppel held Iowa State outdoors records for the mile, two miles, three miles, 3,000 meters and 10,000 meters. She was a five-time Big Eight Conference champion and competed on three national cross-country squads in international competition.

World Records

It was in her last year of collegiate eligibility, 1976, that she set her first world record, a 15-minute, 41.69 second clocking for the three-mile run.

The following year, running for the Iowa State Track Club, Neppel set another world record at the Drake Relays in Des Moines, covering 5,000 meters in 15:52.47.

Her most spectacular performance came at the 1977 Amateur Athletic Union national track championships in Los Angeles where she shattered the women's record for 10,000 meters by 19 seconds, finishing in 33 minutes, 15.09 seconds. All three of her world records have since been broken.

Retired From Competition

Neppel had achieved all that was possible in women's long-distance running. She retired from competition.

"We could see no prospects whatsoever at that time for long-distance running in the Olympics," recalled Murray, her coach. "Peg was getting ready to embark on a Ph.D. program. She felt if she was going to do it justice she had to make a commitment."

Soon after it was learned that a women's marathon race was to be a part of the 1984 Olympics in Los Angeles, Neppel began planning a comeback. But she had been feeling a persistent pain in her abdomen, and went to see her gynecologist, who scheduled surgery the next day.

The doctors found a widespread, rapidly growing cancer. Darrah, who by this time was married to Neppel, was told his wife probably had no more than a month to live.

Worked With Doctors

Peggy's first reaction was that she would not be able to bear children. She told Mark she knew his parents were looking forward to grandchildren.

"Here's a girl with widespread carcinoma, 30 days to live, and she's worried about giving my parents grandkids," he said.

As trained scientists, both Darrahs worked closely with her doctors to understand and control the cancer. Peggy's ability to cope astounded some of her friends. She rode her bicycle to many chemotherapy sessions. After the treatments made her hair fall out, she seemed almost proud of her bald head, and she offered to remove her wig one day for the secretary at her Iowa State office.

"What could you say?" asked Julie Johnson, the secretary. "She was bald, but she was still your friend."

Mark recalled Peggy's thinking about her hair. "She used to say 'The biggest thing Mark and I used to argue about was the style of my hair. Now that my hair's gone, we're more in love.' "

The chemotherapy was successful for about two months before Peggy suffered a relapse, which paralyzed one side of her face. Working with the couple, doctors established a new program of chemotherapy and radiation treatments, which helped alleviate the facial paralysis.

Peggy then went back to the initial chemotherapy program, but with disastrous results. Her facial paralysis returned, she suffered a loss of muscle coordination and a weakening in her legs, and she developed a breast tumor. Doctors tried a new approach, administering two chemotherapy programs simultaneously.

Her breast tumor receded, but her general health was slipping.

"We ran into the problem of not being able to give her enough chemotherapy to kill the cancer and keep her alive at the same time," Mark said.

Peggy began showing neurological problems—a tingling in her arms, loss of control of her legs. Baffled by her condition, doctors decided she should seek treatment at an Iowa City hospital.

Mark said that as Peggy left their Ames home in an ambulance she said: "The first thing we'll do when I get home is to call the adoption agency and start working on getting some kids."

She never came home again.

Hugged Good-Bye

Peggy probably prolonged her life through force of sheer will. But in the end, the cancer grew stronger. Mark said they both knew the end was coming when they saw a blood sample as brown as his leather coat.

They hugged good-bye in the isolation ward where she spent her last week, and Mark returned to Ames.

He said at that point it seemed as though she was living only for him, and by his leaving he gave her his permission to die.

The next day, October 16, after a series of complications resulting in pneumonia, Peggy Neppel Darrah died.

At her memorial service, Ron Whitmer of Ames, an Episcopal priest and the couple's pastor, related a vision Mark experienced at the moment he heard the news by telephone. Whitmer retold the story later to a reporter:

"He said, 'All I could see was Peggy heading toward a great deal of light. And just as she was rounding a corner, there was our first dog, Gretchen, and there were her running shoes. She put on her shoes and she and Gretchen went running.'"

"And he said, 'Peggy was free, she was whole, and the wind was blowing through her hair.'"

Two days later, on a bitterly cold, windy Sunday afternoon, about 500 people showed up for a benefit road race here to help pay for Peggy Neppel Darrah's medical expenses. Mark Darrah started the runners by saying:

"If you're here to watch, Peg stands beside you. If you're here to jog, Peg glides beside you. If you're here to race, Peg's spirit eternally runs with you."

With that he handed the starter the starting gun, took up the leash of their dog, Gretchen II, and took off on the 10-kilometer race.

The benefit raised more than $20,000, and contributions are still coming in to Iowa State's animal science department, which organized the event. After the bills are paid, Mark Darrah said, the rest of the money will go to establish scholarships in his wife's name.

Chapter 11

LIFE AFTER SPORTS

An important aspect of survival is how good you feel about yourself. Sometimes individuals feel good about themselves only when they are participating in sports. They feel bad about themselves when competing in nonathletic activities. Unfortunately, the stories of strong body but weak mind athletes are not jokes to these individuals. The thought of illiterate varsity athletes is indelibly printed in their minds. If you want to be successful in the world of work, you must not think of yourself as a dumb jock. You certainly do not become a successful athlete by being dumb.

As a group, athletes are very similar to their nonathlete agemates in scholastic potential. Differences show up when athletes believe they cannot excel in the classroom, and therefore stop competing for scholastic honors. Instead, they set their sights on merely passing required courses. That is, they no longer strive for As and Bs and settle for Cs and Ds. As in any competitive situation, if an individual believes that he or she cannot excel and, therefore, does not try to excel, the outcome is predictable: that person becomes a loser. You must realize that you can do well in, and outside, the classroom. But belief is not enough. You must work at doing well.

SELF IMAGE

Some athletes also think of themselves as being a lower species of animal. This is understandable when we become aware of the various terms sportswriters and coaches use to describe athletes. Strong athletes are called "bulls," "hogs," and "studs." Fast athletes are called "deer," "greyhounds," and "gazelles," while cagey athletes are referred to as "foxes." It does not take many seasons of being referred to by these terms before a young athlete believes that he or she is indeed an animal. Some brainwashed athletes even behave and smell like their animal prototypes. You must continually tell yourself: "I am not an animal. I am a human being, and I will behave as a human being."

It is also important to realize that you communicate the kind of person you are by the way you dress, walk and talk. Long before you speak, most people form an impression of you. Therefore, if you want people to form a positive impression of you, dress neatly, be well groomed, and look pleasant. Student-athletes represent their team, school, state, and family. It is your responsibility to project a positive public image as an athlete and a student.

Few athletes live in dirty, filthy homes but many of them feed their minds dirty, filthy thoughts and substances. Negative thoughts can immobilize you and mind-altering drugs can destroy you. The "secret" to success is really not a secret: *You must believe in yourself and do nothing that will diminish you as a person.* Individuals who can memorize complex plays and intricate game strategies without putting themselves down or taking drugs that wear them down are also capable of learning math formulae and historical data without devaluing themselves or taking drugs.

Try to keep your classroom and athletic performances in perspective. No scholastic or athletic accomplishment will add to or subtract from your net worth as a person if you put forth your best effort. Instead of using their minds, some athletes lose them to psychedelic drugs that weaken their ability to cope with life. Instead of building their bodies, some athletes tear them down with drugs. When this happens, they cut short their careers as athletes and scholars. For these individuals, life after sports is a dreary, degrading existence.

Some athletes do not understand that the question "Who am I?" is not the same as "What am I?" *Who* refers to you as a unique being, e.g., John Doe. *What* refers to the various roles you play, e.g., football player, student, and citizen. You are not an athlete. Rather, you are an individual who performs as an athlete. You will not end when your playing days end. Wise athletes think of themselves as actors and actresses. They do not think of themselves as being the athletic roles they play. When a game ends—and all games end, so too do their athletic roles. Instead of playing other roles, too many individuals behave as though they are still performing in their sport. Plan ahead so that when your playing days end, you can shift to new roles.

Frequently, athletes who are members of ethnic minority groups confuse their ethnicity with their selves. You are not black or white, for example. You are a person who happens to have been born black or white. You cannot alter the ethnic group you were born into, but you can alter the kind of ethnic group person you are. If you are a member of an ethnic minority, do not let other people shame you into feeling inferior to nonminority persons. Conversely, if you are a member of an ethnic majority group, do not believe that you are superior to minority group persons because of your group identity. Inferiority and superiority are based on performance, not ethnicity. And so too is the quality of your character.

Many people will use your behavior or achievements as barometers of your ethnic group's abilities. Whether you like it is not the issue. You *are* a representative of your race or ethnic group. You should carry this burden with realistic self-expectations. You do not have to be a superstar in your sport or academic courses but you should be courteous and conscientious. *It is your responsibility to be the best person possible.* It is not your responsibility to make up for the misdeeds of other members of your ethnic group.

If you are fortunate, you will feel good about who you are and what you do in and out of sports. While it is important that other people like you, it is more important that you like yourself. Student-athletes who do not realize their potential seldom feel good about themselves.

You must be your own best critic because friends and fans usually are poor judges of your performances. The same people who cheer you for a half-hearted but grandstanding effort that fails may boo you for an all-out effort that results in a score. You must push public cheers and boos into the background so that you can honestly evaluate your athletic performances. This should also be done in the classroom. A grade of C earned with an all-out effort is a better scholastic performance than a B earned by guessing. The object of participating in sports and academics is to realize your maximum learning potential.

It is not enough to take care of your body. You must take care of your mind too. Do not do anything to diminish your ability to think and act in a responsible manner. In summary, we encourage you to use your mind and build your body as preparation for earning a living. A few of you will become professional athletes.

IF YOU BECOME A PROFESSIONAL ATHLETE

Some athletes believe the first financial contract they sign will be a professional contract. Wrong! The first contract most athletes sign is a letter of intent to play for a specific college or university. In addition to calculating the athletic skills you will take to a school, you should determine what you will get in return. This means that you should be concerned with more than room, board, tuition, transportation, and spending money. You should select a school that will provide you with an opportunity (1) to graduate with marketable nonathletic skills and (2) to improve your athletic abilities.

If you aspire to a professional sports contract after college, select a school that will offer you the best training program, media exposure, and business preparation. The impersonal nature of athletic organizations—amateur and professional—is similar to any other business. Athletes are temporary employees. Each athlete must earn more for an organization than he or she is paid. Otherwise, the athlete is an economic liability, and organizations do not like to keep liabilities. This is also true in nonrevenue sports where athletes are expected to pay off in terms of good public relations and school morale rather than ticket sales and television contracts. You should try to enroll in a school that treats its athletes as people rather than chattel property or performing animals. The latter schools will use you and then discard you.

A Marketing Concept

You should develop a marketing concept for yourself. Marketing or selling your athletic skills is the same as selling consumer products to customers. In the case of sports, the athlete is the product to be marketed, the school or professional organization is the company, and the sport is the market. Most athletes do not properly market themselves for several reasons, including the following:

- Lack of initiative.
- Poor planning.
- Inadequate knowledge of the product (themselves).
- Lack of proper training.
- Low personal goals.
- Inadequate knowledge of the market.
- Inadequate knowledge of the company.

Athletes tend to have big egos, but few have adequate humility. It is difficult for some athletes to admit there is something about themselves that needs changing or improvement. Yet it is this kind of introspection and honesty that will help you to improve as a student and an athlete. Select a college that has professional counselors and advisors who will assist in your product analysis and development.

You should know your strengths and weaknesses. This requires periodic inventories of your athletic and academic abilities. Even the best student-athletes can improve. There is no adequate substitute for properly planned, repetitive skill development. It is better to learn your mistakes in practice than to make them during a meet or a game. College is an excellent place to prepare for sports and nonsports careers.

Successful athletes do not leave decisions about their careers to other persons—not parents, coaches, counselors, or friends. It is easy for you to let someone else decide what you should do. But it is not always easy for you to live with their decisions. Remember that it is your life, and making career decisions is too important to leave to others. The same is true for signing a job contract. Confer with other persons, but reserve the final decision for yourself. This will not guarantee that you will be happy with the decisions you make, but they will be *your decisions*. Career decisions should be made selfishly.

From a purely financial perspective, it is bad business for high school or college athletes to accept money or other gifts for themselves or loved ones. A $6,000 or $10,000 car, for example, is a poor trade off for the loss of college eligibility. Similarly, money to sign with a school or to transfer to another one will seem like pennies to the athlete who gets caught. In terms of cold cash, the loss of a college scholarship can be worth $40,000 to $70,000 and the loss of a possible professional contract contingent on college development can be millions of dollars. The "poor but honest" game is not nearly as ridiculous as the "illegal and caught" game. In summary, do not sell yourself cheaply or prematurely.

Before You Sign

We are not attorneys and neither are most athletes. When dealing with legal matters, it is wise to retain an attorney. It is also wise to be familiar with contracts. Simply stated, a contract is any agreement or promise that is legally enforceable. For the professional athlete, this means that in exchange for his or her performance in a sport, a team will pay a specific salary. If you do not understand *everything* in a contract, do not sign it. In some contracts, the large print gives money and the small print takes it away.

Social pressure will make it difficult for you not to immediately sign a contract if you are drafted. This is especially true if you come from a low-income family. Whatever your background, the pressure will be very strong to sign and get the bonus. It probably will be difficult to reject an initial contract offer if all of your teammates who have been drafted have signed their contracts. After years of being conditioned to finish first, it will be hard for you to be last in signing a professional contract. Your financial security, not quickness in signing, is the best goal. Therefore, take your time and sign the best contract that you and your agent can negotiate.

Instead of focusing only on the round in which you were drafted, carefully determine your projected net worth to the team as a player. For example, assume that you are a linebacker picked in the seventh round of the National Football League draft. This does not necessarily mean that you are worth only a seventh round bonus and salary. If you are a student of the game, you know (1) how you compare with other players drafted, especially linebackers, (2) what positions need shoring up on the team that drafted you, and (3) the salary range for your position. The organization will get its money's worth out of you. Your job is to get what you are worth out of the organization.

Baring a spectacular career, your relative salary position on the team will not change very much. Unless you are a superstar, the first contract you sign will determine your income in relationship to your peers for the rest of your career. If your first contract is for $70,000 a year with graduated increases to $150,000 the fourth year, for example, you are not likely to earn more than a teammate who signs the same year you do for $100,000 with graduated increases to $200,000 the fourth year.

It is a common practice for rookies to sign their contracts and buy expensive consumer goods almost before the ink is dry. At this time, they are most vulnerable to overspending. The first mistake is for them to believe newspaper clippings describing them as "millionaires." Unless their contracts are for $1 million a year, they are not millionaires. Less than 10 percent of all professional athletes are bona fide millionaires. A four-year contract for a total of $1 million will not make you a millionaire. If you sign such a contract, you are, at least, a $250,000 a year person, and you should budget accordingly. Remember that the Internal Revenue Service will get its share—one way or another. And so too will your agent.

Our final advice to individuals who become professional athletes is a simple reminder: If you do not have one, devise a basic budget. You should budget your money as carefully as we have tried to get you to budget your time. Your basic budget should include survival and luxury spending. *Survival items* include food, clothing, housing, transportation, health and education. Only after these items are budgeted should *luxury items* be added—recreation, gifts and contributions, savings, and investments. With proper management, the money you earn as a professional athlete can be used to build lifetime security for you and your family.

It takes an average of fourteen years (20,000 hours of practice and 25 injuries) for an athlete to mature from an amateur to a professional. Few make it to the pros. And it takes only one key injury to end an athletic career. Yet, too many athletes behave as if they will play competitive sports for the rest of their lives. Unfortunately, these individuals believe there is no meaningful life after sports. Too few star athletes hear the rapidly approaching footsteps of the next generation coming to take their place in the sun. The average career of a professional basketball or football player is five years.

Most athletic careers do not terminate in professional sports. On the contrary, amateur athletes burn out. Sports cease being fun or rewarding to many participants long before they reach their full athletic potential. Most individuals drop out of sports after high school, and the next largest group drops out in college.

BURNOUT

The longer an individual is an athlete, the fewer things he or she tends to do with nonathletes. Participation in sports can monopolize your time. Slowly the gap widens between you and your nonathlete friends. The socially destructive effect of practicing and participating in sports often culminates in loneliness, anger, and despair. The inability of athletes to adjust to the rigors of their sport can lead to *burnout*—the syndrome of emotional exhaustion and cynicism that occurs after long hours of varsity or professional practice and competition.

In some cases, burnout results in athletes becoming chemically dependent or mentally maladjusted. Under the strain of striving for athletic excellence, an individual's inner resources may be consumed as if by fire, leaving a great emptiness inside. Contrary to many of their wishes or fantasies, athletes are not superhuman. Yet, there are countless instances of athletes who have pushed themselves to physical and emotional breakdowns. To burn out in a sport is to lose interest it it.

It is erroneous to assume that burnout will disappear if you ignore it. There are some clear signs that may suggest burnout: unusual irritability, anger, listlessness, and fatigue. Social symptoms include (1) avoiding practice, (2) a feeling of failure, (3) avoiding contact with friends, and (4) looking forward to the season ending. Physical reactions to psychological stress centering on sports include (1) migraine headaches, (2) a rash of injuries, and (3) excessive diarrhea, salivation or dryness of the mouth, and hearburn.

Unlike romanticized stories and television dramas, being a successful athlete is a tedious, hard job. We are not talking about isolated individuals who suffer burnout alone. Burnout almost always affects other people—teammates, friends, relatives, and fans. Parents in particular carry the "burden" of a child burning out in a sport. Often, it was parents who pushed the individual into a competitive sport and sustained him or her in it. Sometimes burning out is the result of children deciding that they no longer want to fulfill their parents' dreams of athletic glory.

There are several ways you can avoid burnout. Most athletes do not do enough for themselves. Prolonged stress centering on participating in sports can affect your personal life away from sports. It can make you unhappy with your loved ones, unable to be happy during "free" times, and leave you generally without a nonathletic life. You must learn to pay attention to physical symptoms, to put athletic goals in proper perspective, and to understand the nature of burnout. Only then can you control athletic activities, rather than allowing them to control you. As in any job, individuals who work in a sport must learn to vary it, share it and, ultimately, leave it. Nothing lasts forever.

There are two reliable cures for burnout: closeness and being innerdirected. Before you can achieve closeness with others, you have to achieve it with yourself. Athletes who burn out seldom spend enough time with themselves in a constructive manner. Closeness is anywhere and with anyone you choose. Innerdirectedness is not being selfish; rather, it is taking time out for your own self. The purpose, of course, is to do things that are good for your renewal. You should watch for tiredness and pay attention to physical symptoms such as colds or nagging pains. Also you should monitor yourself for shifts in attitude, especially toward self-doubt or self-pity. There are many other things you can do to prevent burnout, including the following: (1) Learn to ask for help. (2) Be aware of your strengths and weaknesses. (3) Take time out for recreation. (4) Don't feel guilty if you have not lived up to your ideal of a superathlete. (5) Learn a survival skill not associated with sports. (6) Set realistic goals for yourself.

Self-Directed Persons

The question is: How can you become self-directed outside sports? There are four basic components to self-direction. First, you must believe that self-direction is important. You must not simply give lip service to controlling your life, you must practice it. Self-direction works only if it is a living concept; it must be given as much practice as subject matter recitals in school. We learn by doing and most people learn best by planning and carrying out their own life goals. Being involved in athletics has given you a good foundation. You have learned to set realistic goals and to work hard to achieve them.

Second, you must cope with adversity. Too many athletes are sheltered from adversity. Parents, academic advisors, and coaches frequently pull strings to get them out of trouble. Whenever this happens, athletes do not become responsible for resolving their own problems. Responsibility and self-direction are learned only by seizing opportunities to succeed and fail on your own merit. If you believe in your inadequcy to handle stressful nonathletic situations, you will become dependent on other people to save you. There is nothing wrong with seeking help, but it is not growth-producing for you to seek the assistance of others before trying to resolve a problem yourself. Individuals who become totally dependent on other persons for problem-resolution lag behind their peers in social and business survival skills.

Third, you should maintain an experimental attitude. When given an opportunity to try new behaviors, do not become alarmed or disappointed if you make mistakes. Knowing what not to do is just as important as knowing what to do in specific situations. It is not easy to accept mistakes, since most organizations are built on doing things correctly. Mistakes in sports are seldom rewarded and for this reason you may have to learn new ways to view experimental behavior. Individuals fearful of making mistakes will seldom risk trying new things. Without trying, self-direction, independence, and creativity cannot be discovered.

Fourth, if you do not know it, you must learn the meaning of responsibility. The implications of the decisions you make must be understood. You will not always make the correct response—nobody does—but you should always accept responsibility for your behavior. This does not mean hiding behind your coach or parents if you do something that may have unpleasant consequences. The mark of truly mature persons is the ability to accept both the good and bad consequences of their behavior. Often, the only punishment is admitting that you were in error. In other instances, it may require accepting a loss of time, money, a passing grade, or a job.

There is much talk about external pressures that affect nonathletes. Although nonathletes complain about things that bother them, they often think that athletes have no problems. More than anything else, athletes are pressured to succeed—to win a place on the team, to achieve passing grades in their classes, to hold their own in athletic contests, and to be happy. Frequently, fans expect athletes to adhere to a higher standard of morality than the general population.

You cannot escape from all pressures, and it is not desirable that you do. A certain amount of pressure acts as a driving force, kindling the desire to finish a job or task and go on to the next activity. In short, pressure is what drives successful people. But there are differences between constructive and destructive pressures. Constructive pressure is based on adequate motivation and personal reward or satisfaction through achievement. In and out of sports, when an individual does not feel a degree of positive achievement, distress and defeat will result. In order to live successfully with external pressure, you must first know how and when to exert internal pressure.

Pressure applied for its own sake or for a perverted reason ("to punish yourself and thereby become tough") will almost always inflict harm. Nor should you push yourself to achieve a goal without understanding it. If you nag yourself to do better in an activity without understanding exactly what it is you must do, you will end up becoming more distressed. Pressure is positive only when it is combined with cues that improve your knowledge. Finally, if you are to be creative, external pressure is not the answer. Coaches cannot teach certain natural moves that gifted athletes make nor can teachers and employers teach the creative ways individuals get certain results. Creativity comes from within each of us. You must be as willing to develop it off the playing field as on it.

GET A GOOD JOB

Learn your subjects well in college so that you can get a good job. If you have an opportunity to work during off-seasons, especially summers, take advantage of it. Work is more than a means through which we can buy consumer goods. Through legal, acceptable work we purchase our dignity and the respect of other people. Also through work we achieve identity and social status. There is little social status in being an unemployed ex-athlete.

Involvement with meaningful work is an adult activity. Participating in sports is a form of work, but it is a very temporary activity. It is not that we *work* when we become adults; rather, we work *to become* adults. Meaningful work provides a much needed transition from childhood to adulthood. Furthermore, it is a fundamental economic reality—most people work in order to provide financial support for themselves and their family. Finally, work has a social reality. It is through work that people earn their place in communities and develop within themselves a sense of accomplishment. You should not depend solely on sports to provide these things.

Grave psychological disturbances can result when former athletes are unable to get a good job. In these instances, the time spent in athletics becomes a handicap. There is little demand in nonsports jobs for catching or hitting balls or knocking people down. As an athlete, you can do much more than the things required by a coach. You must develop your other potential skills in the academic classrooms. Too many former athletes did not do this. And they are stuck in low-paying, dead-end jobs, if any at all.

Sports are temporary but academic/vocational knowledge lasts forever. If you graduate from college without a nonsport marketable skill, you have wasted a golden opportunity to become something more than an athlete. Throughout this book, we have encouraged you to use your athletic scholarship to get the best education possible. If you do, your life after sports can be as meaningful as your life in sports.

KEEPING YOUR BALANCE

This has been our message to people who participate in competitive sports: Your life need not be considerably different than that of other people because you participate in sports. We acknowledge, and it has been discussed in previous chapters, that athletics impose limitations that may require special attention. However, at the other end of the continuum—and equally wrong—is the idea that you have to be Mr. or Ms. Superathlete in order to be a success. On the contrary, you are entitled to be as average as people without a sports background.

Survival places similar demands on both athletes and nonathletes, requires sacrifices of them and, therefore, provides both groups with the same basic rights and responsibilities. When discussing your rights as an athlete, we have focused, first, on what you are entitled to as a person; second, on what you are entitled to as a student-athlete; and, third, on what you will need when your playing days are over. For, indeed, in and out of sports you will play a myriad of social roles. Obviously, you will be a better citizen if you are adequately educated and gainfully employed. It is the right of every student-athlete to receive education that will lead to the full development of his or her mind and body and to be completely emancipated from all forms of second-class citizenship.

No matter how much you may prefer to be protected and supported by other persons, nor how much they desire to do so, you are ultimately the master of your own life. Accordingly, each master must be the captain and engineer during his or her journey through life. In nautical terms, this means plotting a course, gauging the social climate, and knowing when and in what direction to travel. Parents, coaches, teammates, and other persons are crew members who can help you do some of the many chores needed to successfully reach your destination—but it is neither their career nor their life.

Each of us comes into this world alone under circumstances unlike those of any other person. True, there are similarities in birth, but each birth is a unique happening. And when we die, we leave this world alone—under circumstances peculiar to ourselves. The time that you spend between birth and death is your unique experience. There can never be a similar combination of nurture and nature. You should make the most of your opportunities in and out of sports. Through your accomplishments you will be recognized as an individual, judged and treated on merit. Millions of former athletes have proven that they can equal other persons in thought, art, science, literature, and other cultural achievements. What will you prove?

Sports provide an opportunity for the participants to test their character and temperament as well as their courage and fortitude. Some of the things you find out about yourself in college will be unpleasant, while other things will be both surprising and pleasant. In many ways, sports can be a valuable preparation for nonsports activities. Check all the statements listed below that summarize the values you exhibit while playing sports.

- ☐ Respect for other persons.
- ☐ Self-discipline.
- ☐ Self-confidence.
- ☐ Self-understanding.
- ☐ Self-respect.
- ☐ Loyalty to teammates.
- ☐ Responsibility for your own behavior.

☐ Emotional control during stressful situations.
☐ Improved communication skills.
☐ Honesty when other people are dishonest.
☐ Ability to come back stronger after losses.
☐ Ability to lead others.
☐ Humility.

If you checked seven or more of the items listed above, it is highly likely that you will have a happy, productive life when your playing days are over. The more items you checked, the better your chances to live life after sports with a minimum of emotional distress. If you do not have an identity outside sports, it is crucial that you develop one as soon as possible. Always keep in mind the fact that only a few of the millions of persons who reach for athletic stardom will actually achieve it. And the sports time of those few who do achieve athletic stardom will consume only a small fraction of their lives. We encourage you to prepare for nonathletic competition as carefully as you prepare to become an All-American. You may or may not become an All-American but you will become an ex-athlete. Proper planning can culminate in rewards equal to or greater than any you can achieve in sports.

BIBLIOGRAPHY

Academic Preparation for College—What Students Need to Know and Be Able to Do. New York: The College Board, 1983.

Action for Excellence—A Comprehensive Plan to Improve Our Nation's Schools. Washington, D.C.: Task Force on Education for Economic Growth of the Education Commission of the States, 1983.

American Council on Education, "NCAA Convention To Vote On Major Sports Legislation," *Higher Education and National Affairs.* 32:35, 3, December 16, 1983.

Blaylock, Mabry G. *How to Study and Like It: Orientation to Learning.* Los Angeles: Crescent, 1973.

Brandt, Phillip L., Meara, Naomi, and Schmidt, Lyle D. *A Time to Learn: A Guide to Academic and Personal Effectiveness.* New York: Holt, Rinehart and Winston, 1974.

Brown, William F. and Holtzman, Wayne H. *A Guide to College Survival.* Englewood Cliffs, NJ: Prentice-Hall, 1972.

Caldwell, Louis P. *After the Tassel Is Moved: Guidelines for High School Graduates.* Grand Rapids, MI: Baker Book House, 1979.

Carnes, Ralph L. and Carnes, Valerie. *The Essential College Survival Handbook: An Insider's Guide to Making College Work for You.* New York: Playboy Press, 1981.

Edwards, Harry. "The Black 'Dumb Jock'—An American Sports Tragedy," *The College Board Review.* 131: Spring, 1984.

Fiske, Edward B. *The New York Times Selective Guide to Colleges.* New York: Times Books, 1982.

Goals for College Success—A Practical Reference for College Preparation. Austin, TX: Texas College and University System Coordinating Board, 1983.

Graesser, Arthur C. *Prose Composition Beyond the Word.* New York: Springer-Verlag, 1981.

Hawes, Gene R. *Hawes' Comprehensive Guide to Colleges.* New York: New American Library, 1978.

Interassociational Presidents' Committee on Collegiate Athletics. "Athletics As Education: A Policy Statement," *Higher Education and National Affairs.* 33:14, 3, July, 1984.

Lock, Corey. *Study Skills.* West Lafayette, IN: Kappa Delta Pi, 1981.

Manski, Charles F. and Wise, David A. *College Choice in America.* Cambridge, MA: Harvard University Press, 1983.

McClintock, John. *100 Top Colleges: How to Choose and Get In.* New York: Wiley, 1982.

Mitchell, Joyce S. *The Guide to College Life.* Englewood Cliffs, NJ: Prentice-Hall, 1968.

Morgan, Clifford T. and Deese, James. *How to Study.* New York: McGraw-Hill, 1969.

Pauk, Walter. *How to Study in College.* Boston: Houghton Mifflin, 1974.

Peterson's Annual Guide to Undergraduate Study. Princeton, NJ: Peterson's Guides, 1984.

Phillips, Anne G. and Sotiriou, Peter E. *Steps to Reading Proficiency: Preview Skimming, Rapid Reading, Skimming and Scanning, Critical and Study Reading.* Belmont, CA: Wadsworth, 1982.

Pivar, William H. *The Whole Earth Textbook: A Survival Manual for Students.* Philadelphia: W. B. Saunders, 1978.

Pope, Loren. *The Right College: How to Get In, Stay In, or Get Back In.* New York: Macmillan, 1982.

Preparing the High School Student for College. Baton Rouge, LA: Louisiana Board of Regents, 1982.

Raygor, Alton L. and Wark, David M. *Systems for Study.* New York: McGraw-Hill, 1980.

Richard, John A. *How to Make Better Grades.* New York: A. S. Barnes, 1964.

Shepherd, James F. *The Houghton Mifflin Study Skills Handbook.* Boston: Houghton Mifflin, 1982.

Staton, Thomas F. *How to Study.* Montgomery, AL: How To Study, 1968.

Steil, Lyman K., Barker, Larry L., and Watson, Kittie W. *Effective Listening: Key to Your Success.* Reading, MA: Addison-Wesley, 1983.

The College Handbook. New York: The College Board, 1983.

University College Catalog. Norman, OK: University of Oklahoma, 1984.

Voeks, Virginia. *On Becoming an Educated Person: Orientation to College Life.* Philadelphia: Saunders, 1979.

Walker, Marion E. and Beach, Mark. *Making It in College.* New York: Mason-Charter, 1976.

Walter, Tim and Siebert, Al. *Student Success.* New York: Holt, Rinehart and Winston, 1984.

Zemsky, Robert and Oedel, Penney. *The Structure of College Choice.* New York: The College Board, 1984.

INDEX